From Assistant
Fetish Priest
to Archbishop

FROM ASSISTANT FETISH PRIEST TO ARCHBISHOP

Studies in Honour of Archbishop Dery

Edited
by
Paul Bemile

VANTAGE PRESS
New York / Atlanta
Los Angeles / Chicago

Contents

Preface

To give a fitting honour to a man who rose from assistant fetish priest to archbishop is certainly not a task for amateurs. For Archbishop Peter Poreku Dery as a man, a Christian, a priest and a bishop has made a very great impact on the Church in Ghana, especially during his twenty-five years as a bishop. Even now that he is the president of the Ghana Bishops Conference, a member of the Standing Committee of SECAM, and a member of the Pontifical Laity Council, Archbishop Dery still recalls with nostalgia his day of baptism in Jirapa in 1933, his ordination to the priesthood in 1951 at Nandom, and his maiden work as bishop in his native diocese of Wa, which he built up from scratch. It was not without reluctance that he left his diocese to take over the episcopal see of Tamale in 1975.

A festschrift to honour such a one who has worked very hard as a bishop for twenty-five years should have been the prerogative of notable scholars, cardinals, and bishops, all of whom he has met and charmed. While there is some validity in this observation, other factors need to be taken into consideration. Our episcopal jubilarian completely refused to have his priestly ordination celebrated in *choro et in refectorio*. Will he now accept a big fanfare by way of an elaborate festschrift? But being a full-fledged

Dagao, he might be ready to accept a small token gift from the Northern Diocesan Priests Association of which he is the founding father.

Since we know that he can accept pleasant surprises, six amateurs in the name of the Northern Diocesan Priests Association are venturing to present the following articles in view of commemorating the twenty-five years of Archbishop Dery's episcopal ordination.

"As the kernel and centre of his Good News, Christ proclaims salvation, this great gift of God which is liberation from everything that oppresses man but which is above all liberation from sin and the Evil One, in the joy of knowing God and being known by him, of seeing him and being given over to him" *(Evangelii Nuntiandi* 9). These words of the synodal document aptly sum up Father Albert A. Kuuire's article "The Dimension of Christian Salvation," which opens the series of articles intended as a legacy of Archbishop Peter Poreku Dery.

If he were asked to recall his childhood, Archbishop Dery would probably have begun like this: "I am a native of Zimoopare, a village in Dagaabaland in the Upper West Region of Ghana. I was born in about 1918 of pagan parents in Ngmankurinaa's house. Since I was born after the death of my immediate brother, I was thought to be a reincarnation of my brother and was thus called Dery. At a rather early age, I used to accompany my uncle, Ngmankurinaa, to establish his many and varied fetishes for the prominent people in my area. My main duty was to help my uncle slay the animals and hens required for the establishment of *konkpenebie, konkyekommo, sokyere, doosoglaa, nyogebaliere,* and the rest of them."

Father Joseph W. Apuri continues the story of the assistant fetish priest with his article: "African Parallels for the Jewish Concept and Ritual of Blood." His historical linguistic analysis of the Kassena-Nankanni provides a means for reconstructing a ritual ancestral to groups of genetically related languages in Ghana and Bourkina-Faso.

The saying that God writes straight on crooked lines is best exemplified in the Poreku family. For as Providence would have it, the very people who were steeped in fetishism and preoccupied with the spread of it were instrumental in the spreading of the Good News in Dagaabaland, which stretches from Ghana to Ivory Coast and Bourkina-Faso. Father Lucas Abadamloora in his article, "The Church in West Africa," gives a brief sketch of the foundation of the Church in West Africa and gives his own forecast of the Church of tomorrow. Fatalism, however, does not figure in the personality of our jubilarian.

Archbishop Dery's philosophy of man is quite complex and many faceted. Gifted with a charming personality that is able to attract and influence young and old, rich and poor, black and white, our jubilarian has been able to weave the web of intricate relations that hold together the churches of the Northern Ecclesiastical Province where he is the leader. Maybe his outstanding defect is his continual optimism even in the face of sinful man and a crises-laden world. If this is a sin, it is a happy fault, for it is this Christian attitude to life that sees a gleam of light beyond darkness, a life beyond the grave.

It would therefore not be inaccurate to say that Father Edward B. Tengan's article, "Personalism: A Plea for the Person-Attitude in Life," is a good attempt to recapture Archbishop Dery's philosophy of integral human development.

If the word *inculturation* has generated a flurry of discussions among African liturgists, theologians, and biblicists, it was already being practiced by Archbishop Dery long before Vatican II. The indigenisation of the Liturgy started immediately after his episcopal ordination on 8 May 1960. How wide has been his influence within Ghana, Africa, and elsewhere still remains a question that may never be answered during his lifetime. In any event, the article of Father Paul Bemile on "Some Theological Reflections of Africans after the Independence of Black Africa" is a humble tribute to the man who was and still is a daring pioneer of inculturation.

Appropriately, the amateurs give way to a man of wide repute, the successor of Archbishop Dery, to crown this festschrift. Rt. Reverend Gregory E. Kpiebaya's article, "Shepherd of his Flock," in a humourous but serious way, recounts the twenty-five years of Archbishop Dery's episcopal apostolate. True to his motto, *Apostolus Jesu Christi,* Archbishop Dery is a true apostle of the Lord Jesus Christ and his flock.

Archbishop Dery's long-established belief in the profitability of youth leadership is underscored by Father Yangyuoru's article, "Towards Effective Youth Movement: A Sociological Viewpoint." Not unlike Dery, Yangyuouru advances the thesis that viable Christian youth organizations are, in essence, the sources of both spiritual and social development.

Summing up, it may be said that since God's saving presence is greater than man and the Church, salvation can be mediated by the words and sacrificial deeds of other religions. But since Christ still remains the unique Saviour and the sole mediator between God and man, it is this Word of God, who became man in every way except sin, which has to be proclaimed and preached to all peoples, at all times, and in all cultures whilst paying due respect to the human person and his environment.

Without the suport of several people, this book would never have been completed. I wish to express deep appreciation to the Missionaries of Africa for their work in northern Ghana. I equally gratefully acknowledge the editors of Vantage Press, Father David Goergen of The Missionaries of Africa in Washington, D.C., and Professor Josaphat Kubayanda of the Ohio State University for their gracious assistance in the preparation and production of the manuscript. Needless to say, however, that whatever errors of fact or interpretation this book may contain are the responsibility of the authors.

Paul Bemile

From Assistant Fetish Priest to Archbishop

The Dimensions of Christian Salvation

INTRODUCTION: THE SALVATION OF MAN, A FUNDAMENTAL QUESTION

Man's salvation has always been, and continues to be, with ever greater awareness, the fundamental question both to the human community as a whole and to the individual person.

As our human societies get into an era in which technology and science become dominant, many things that were accepted without or with very little questioning have become subjects of discussion today. And so does the nature itself of our Church. The real mission of the Church and her structures are called into question, and the function of the Church today has become dubious and controversial even for serious thinkers within her very walls. However, whatever vision one makes of our Church today, of its functions and structures, there is this preliminary question on which this vision will be based and that one cannot simply bypass; that is "Man's Salvation."

A modern Dominican Christologist, Ignace Berten, once depicted Christianity as "a venture among many others, seeking an answer to this fundamental question confronting all men."[1]

In fact, this is a question that preoccupies Hinduism, Buddhism, Islamism, and even animism, which is practised among our people, and all religions in general; also scientific theories like Marxism, communism, the different brands of socialism, as well as philosophical theories and histories. All are looking at this same question, the "salvation of Man," although each one may look at it from its own point of view and proposes its own solution, adopting its own particular strategy and structures, using its own "theological" language.

What I propose to share with you in this paper is the result of a personal reflection on this fundamental question on man's salvation made in the light of the salvation that we Catholic Christians are promised in Jesus Christ. So it is not just 'salvation' in all its wide context that we want to discuss here, but we want to limit ourselves to that salvation announced by Jesus Christ in whom we profess our deep belief and to whom we adhere with all the forces that we can marshall in us as human beings.

THE BIBLICAL CONCEPT OF SALVATION

To make a reflection on the salvation announced by Jesus Christ, the idea of salvation developed throughout the history of Israel, the "People of God," seems indispensable. It is only against the background of Israel's conception of salvation that Jesus is seen as the universal Saviour of all men, the Messiah who has been promised by Yahweh the God of Israel and of the Universe.

From the biblical use of the term 'salvation,' when we consider the different situations in which it is used and made to describe, we come to the conclusion that the term can be used in a completely general sense to signify "the setting free" from situations of all kinds of needs that the individual (danger, injustice, sickness) or community (war, political upheaval, famine)[2] may find himself or itself in. This means the liberation of man, either as an individual or as a community, from any of these situations that are alienating him from what would be considered as the integral situation that he longs for as natural to him. And although in the Old Testament the work of salvation is always finally attributed to God himself (Ex. 14:13 and 15:2), this deliverance is also realised by the actual person who has been in that situation from which he needed to be delivered (1 Sm 25:26,31,33).[3] It can also be effected by other men in purely natural circumstances (1 Sm 11:3; 2 Sm 10:11,19);[4] or still, alternatively by men who are seen as instruments in the hands of God.

We must say that for the Jewish people the idea of salvation was also rather vague from the beginning. Starting from what we may call a primitive eudaemonistic optimism, it eventually became idealised as an achievement on a political and national plane; hence the political liberation of the nation from their enemies, for which the age of David was always regarded as the ideal, i.e., salvation in its totality.

With the prophets the concept of salvation developed further into an expectation of a "New Creation" with which the idea of a saved "remnant" was connected. It is with this reality in view that Jeremiah, in the name of Yahweh, could proclaim, "I will give them a heart that they may know that I am Yahweh. They shall be my people and I shall be their God, for they shall return to me with all their heart" (Jer 24:7; see also 31:33, 34; 32:39; and Ez 36:26 ff.). This means that to the saved one "a new heart and a new spirit" will be given. One can say that it was from here that the idea of salvation was pushed to the point that it became a new creation; and though not exclusively, it took also the form of a world that was to come at the end of the present age.

Yet for the prophets, this salvation as a new creation

did not seem to be outside the present age, the age in which they were living, but something that had to take place right there and then. The unfavourable, alienating situations in which the people were living had to change to give place to this new creation.

And this is why the Prophet Amos in particular, who lived before both Jeremiah and Ezekiel, had already condemned, in the name of Yahweh, the corrupted lives of the cities, the false security in which the people were living, and particularly the social injustices that were rife in Israel (Am 3:9–15; 4:1–3).[5]

Amos saw as the only deliverance from such situations to be a conversion (Am 5:14–16); and it is to this conversion, which is the creation of a new situation, that he exhorted the people there and then, saying, "Seek good and not evil, that you may live; and so the Lord, the God of Hosts, will be with you as you have said. Hate evil and love good, and establish justice in the gate; it may be that the Lord, the God of hosts will be gracious to the remnant of Joseph."[6] Such an exhortation is to a real engagement.

This is not only a question of a moral conversion, but a real and concrete transformation of the society that treated the widows unjustly, oppressed the poor, and crushed the needy (Am 4:1 ff.).

Hence a radical change in relating to one another, among the "people of God," is demanded of the Israelite society itself; a change that would make it possible for the widows, the orphans, and all those who had become marginalised in the society, to live in *peace* and *security*.

It remains a fact, however, that in the Old Testament, the idea of salvation, which became only more and more defined through the evolution of time, had always been somehow connected with the expectation of a messianic time: the expectation of an aeon when the people would live in peace and safety in the Kingdom of their God at the end of time. This concept of salvation as the dawning of a messianic period, the coming of a messianic Kingdom, took its start with the prophecy of Nathan to the King, David, (2 Sm 7:3–16), and was picked up and developed by the Prophet Amos (Am 9:11–15), and later pushed to its Old Testament limits by the prophet Isaiah (Is 7:14 ff.).

So, although at the time of the prophets the idea of salvation among the Jews had developed to such a point that the aspect of a messianic and an eschatological expectation, i.e., the coming of a future messiah, a saviour, in the fullness of time, seemed to predominate at certain moments, salvation as a deliverance from the actual situation of an alienation was always present. The prophets continuously called the people to effectively engage in creating this new situation there and then, by converting from their unjust ways of dealing with one another, and from the sense of a false security in which they were living.

They encouraged the people and made them more and more aware of the task of realising this new creation—the bringing about of this new and hoped-for situation in which there would be happiness, peace, and security—for Yahweh was with them to give them a "new heart," and a "new spirit" (Jer 32:39). He would give them a messiah, a prince of peace and of justice, under whose rule there would be a definitive reconciliation (Is 11). Hence it was to be a salvation that would consist in reconciling the actual aberrant situation, and that would attain its final perfection in an eschatological time.

So salvation, which, for all men, is to regain a certain human integrity, finally included, for the Jews, a state that is to be looked forward to, and actively hoped for, an *expectation*.

The New Testament conception of the salvation of man, the Christian salvation—for which we hope—does not start from nothing. It takes over all the important developments of this concept of salvation in the Old Testament, and attaches them to the person of Jesus Christ considered as the one who has come to deliver man from this situation of need, domination, and misery, danger, sickness—both moral and physical—social injustice, famine, and even political oppression. In fact, it is all these that constitute the situation of "nonsalvation," of "insecurity," in which man finds himself, and from which Christ, according to our belief, came at "the fullness of time" to liberate him.

We can say that this is the situation of sin in which man is. Thus Paul, in his letter to Timothy, aptly represented this when he said: "This word is true and worthy of absolute belief: Christ Jesus has come into the world to save the sinners, of whom I am the first" (1 Tm 1:15). Christ the Son of God, and so God Himself, becomes our Saviour; and the knowledge of God (Faith), not knowledge about God (just science), becomes salvation. Before we go on to examine what dimensions then the Christian salvation has, let us take a look at what "natural" man aspires to as salvation.

SALVATION: AN EFFECTIVE ASPIRATION FOR A BETTER SITUATION

If we could make a comparison between our present theological concept of salvation with the concept of salvation as it has been developed throughout the Bible, we would affirm with P. Smulders that there are fragmentary tendencies in it that make us realise that only certain dimensions are chosen and insisted upon to the detriment of all other dimensions that are inherent in the concept.[7]

For example, dimensions like the "future total reconciliation," conversion, resurrection and the future life, in fact, the eschatological aspect of man's salvation; these dimensions have been for too long and so much insisted upon that the actual situation of nonsalvation and of insecurity in which man lives: hunger, political and cultural domination, cultural and material poverty, misery, and the social injustices in which man is, had been relegated to the background if not forgotten. The best theological response we always advocate in the face of such situations of insecurity and of nonsalvation is that the subject in that situation look only to a better future situation, a future salvation; and this attitude and frame of mind makes it not possible for us to do anything that could effectively liberate ourselves or the others found in such inhuman conditions and situations from which they would need to be delivered.

This fragmentary way of looking at salvation, therefore, instead of operating salvation at all for man right now in his situation of misery and nonsalvation, favours and perpetuates this state of nonsalvation, and all because of the passive expectation of the messianic salvation that it inspires. It is, in fact, this one-sided presentation of human salvation that leads Marxism to denounce Christianism, and religion, for that matter, as an opium used for duping the people, since its insistence on the eschatological salvation gets to such a point that even the present inhuman conditions in which men are living are seen as something to be acquiesced in and even sought as guarantee for this eschatological perfect reconciliation.

Assuming, therefore, this fact of the fragmentariness of our theology of salvation, as a reality that is with us and makes any synthesis difficult, the principal reason for the difficulty in the formulation of the desired synthesis can be attributed to the fact that the Christian salvation is a history revealing only gradually and in many forms man's salvation as the will of God, and which historicity, gradual revelation, therefore makes it difficult to make any ethical or philosophical synthesis. This difficulty pointed out is rightly so. As Jakob Obersteiner, who also sees salvation as a history, observes, messianism is "the biblical expectation of an aeon of salvation at the end of time which will culminate in the setting up of a Kingdom of God."[8]

However, it is precisely the element of historicity that adds to the complexity of the nature of salvation, and so makes it difficult to have a synchronic view of it, philosophical or moral. For, any such synchronic view or synthesis would inevitably be partisan to a particular philosophy or ethic belonging to one particular period of history, or history of a particular people and situation. And so such a synthesis would be running the risk of closing the door to other dimensions of the salvation of man, which manifest themselves in the various circumstances all along the human history, or which are particular to a people in a given situation not partisan to the elements in this synthesis.

However, in history, which takes its course, we have the human elements that make it possible to read the main dimensions of our salvation honestly in a given time and conditions, even if a synthesis whatsoever is not immediately possible.

Therefore, without searching absolutely for a synthesis, we could say that, in fact, the question of man's salvation, which is itself the fundamental question, comes back to this other question: WHAT IS MAN? i.e., what is man's identity and what must he do to realise what he should be? So the question of man's salvation is a fundamental one; it is a quest to rejoin an original state of integrity that he feels he should be in but is not. The question put in this manner, philosophically as it may seem, means that man in his present state aspires to a state other than the actual one in which he finds himself. He sees himself in a situation that he feels could have been a better one, and so he aspires to the situation that he believes is better than this actual one.

This better situation, according to Walgrave,[9] is an authenticity, a plenitude, a cerain perfect harmony, which man feels should belong to his nature, but the absence of which he realises in his actual human condition. These qualities of life: his authenticity, plenitude, peace and security, and harmony are not found in the present situation in which man exists.

Therefore, the answer to this question: What is man? is, indeed, the fundamental question to be answered by all who are in quest for man's salvation. And this, in my view, must also be looked for in the existential and concrete circumstances of life that surrounds man, the subject of this salvation.

So the concept of salvation, to borrow from the words of Jacques van Nieuwenhove, is at the same time an experience of a *negativity* and of an *expectation*. That is to say, these two situations are correlative to the concept of salvation:

i)   a negative situation in which man experiences a negation of an ideal reality, a certain inaccomplishment, a nonintegrity, hence a situation of nonsalvation;

ii)   then an expected human situation that would correspond better to man's internal and deep aspirations; the ultimate reality that he thinks he has been created for.

In this light, salvation should not consist then in the ultimate term, the situation perfectly and completely reconciled and conformed to the authentic aspiration of man, but should also include every step that man takes forward in the movement away from this negative situation towards the better situation that will be a perfect representation of his total reconciliation with his profound aspiration: his authentic and primitive human condition of plenitude and harmony.

Whatever the step that leads man out of this situation of nonsalvation and places him on the path towards this authenticity, fullness, and harmony, this step is itself a certain degree of salvation effected, even if it is not yet the final and perfectly accomplished stage itself of salvation arrived at. This movement definitely implies an ethic and a technique that form part of the reality of man but that should differ according to the particular situation and different circumstances in which each society exists, the societies in which men live.

THE CHRISTIAN DIMENSIONS OF SALVATION

We have said above that the Christian Faith, which we can also call the Christian "venture," is considered, especially in our days, by many as just one answer among others to the fundamental question: Man's salvation. As we have also remarked, in the Christian theology, only certain aspects of this salvation have been selected and stressed upon so much so that the other dimensions are left in quasi-oblivion.

The point is, if Christ has come to bring salvation to man, the question may be asked: is it only a partial salvation that he brings or a total one? Does this salvation that he brings apply to only some particular situations of nonsalvation in which man is, or to all situations of sin and nonsalvation that beset man?

If the salvation that Christ has brought to us is the deliverance of man from all situations of nonsalvation, which is indeed the situation of alienation as we have already described it, then how can we reduce this salvation of Christ to only its eschatological dimensions, leaving out the actual situations of alienation in which man exists? If Christ has truly brought salvation to man, it is our belief that it must be salvation in its plenitude. And this seems sufficiently clear when we take Christ himself as "The Message"; i.e., not only what he said but also his whole attitude towards human life, and his personality.

In presenting his message as the Messiah, the one who came to deliver the "helpless" out of their "helplessness" (Mt 11:3–6; see also Is 29:18 ff.; 35:5 ff.; 61:1), Christ proclaimed salvation for the people, especially for the poor (Mt 11:5). He preached a plenitude, a better human condition for men. But for the realisation of this better human condition, which he proclaimed as a Kingdom, "The Kingdom of God" (Mt 5:3 ff.), he demanded faith. This faith is, in fact, necessary for the salvation that he was offering: "He who believes and is baptised will be saved; but he who does not believe will be condemned" (Mt 16:16). Faith here is, therefore, that which opens the door to this Kingdom of God, this better human condition that Jesus came to proffer. It is the cord, the assurance to man that what he aspires to as a possibility will, indeed, become a reality; man will ultimately and perfectly be reconciled to himself.

This faith does not consist only in the assurance that what is possible will become real, but it is also a decision for Christ himself (Mt 12:30) who thus becomes the salvation of man and the presence of this Kingdom among men. On this level, one can say that in proclaiming this Kingdom, Christ really presented it as an eschatological event, something that is for the future, the heavenly kingdom where the peace of paradise will be brought back (Is

11:6 ff.), a utopia; but a utopia that is, nevertheless, credible because of Christ himself.

However, in the very core of this proclamation of the kingdom, Christ never ceased to wage a relentless battle against the alienated human conditions of his time, the evils of the then actual condition in which he found people. His preaching and activities were geared towards delivering man from the situations of oppression, hunger, sickness, etc., in which man actually was. He sought to create a community in which justice could be a reality there and then among the people. The kingdom is already present and all are called to it through faith and conversion (Mk 1:15). Christ announces this eschatological kingdom as something close at hand indeed, even imminent; a reality the existence of which can be detected and which is already active and at work among men; something that brings salvation and that forces man to come to a decision at whatever point of history in which he finds himself. As Rudolf Schnackenburg says, all this is bound up with the person and mission of Christ himself. "In him the Old Testament's prophecies are fulfilled."[10]

The concrete healings, the feedings, and the appeasement of the guilty consciences of the people that Christ was operating were therefore not only a sign, but an actual and effective creation of better situations, and so, of better conditions of living for at least those who benefitted from them. He was actually delivering them from their situations of want, and obtaining for them what they were yearning for—healings of their ailments. He fed them, (Mt 14:13–21); he healed them (Mt 15:29–31, and parallel texts), and besides that he condemned the injustices and hypocritical attitudes of their leaders, which were preventing the coming and realisation of the Kingdom among them there and then (Mt 23:13 ff.); the Kingdom that brings salvation and is itself salvation to man.

From all that has been said above, I think that one can sincerely conclude with the surety of faith that Christ is the climax and the synthesis of the totality of salvation as developed throughout the Bible. In him is present the kingdom of God with all its saving elements. He is himself the promise of the eschatological times, but his ministry there and then also revealed the actual presence of this promise among men and assured its full accomplishment in the future.

Thus, taking the totality of Christ's ministry and preaching, particularly his Resurrection, it appears absolutely impossible to deny in all sincerity that the works Christ performed were already an authentic salvation obtained there and then for the people in situations that were alienations of the authentic human conditions, even if these situations in which those people were living were only particular to them.

It is only in the message of Christ, therefore, that there is found an answer to all the different dimensions of the salvation for which man is in earnest quest, even though this message was given within the cultural background of a particular people living in situations peculiar to them. The salvation proffered by Christ is not just a salvation only realisable in the future, and so to which man just simply aspires in faith and hope; surely, there is a dimension of it, the eschatological dimension of it, in which man must continue to have faith and to hope; but to think that this salvation promised and offered by Christ is only realisable in the future, would be a simple reduction of the faith, preached by Christ, to a scientific explanation of events in history. And such a reduction of the faith would be, as Jacques van Nieuwenhove calls it, "an inflation of the faith which would neglect the actual human circumstances of non-plenitude, non-harmony and non-identity; in short, it is the situation of non-salvation itself from which man wants and ardently hopes to be delivered."

Furthermore, we can say that the series of evangelical elements brought to light by the message of Christ do not only reveal the kingdom as the optimum situation of salvation, and to which he calls all men. He also, through this message, reveals the *love* of God the Father himself as the source of *reconciliation,* hence the source of this profound identity of himself that man is looking for in the bottom of himself, identity with his genuine and primitive nature. That is why the salvation of man, if it has to be the full salvation, cannot evade communion with this *other reality,* which is *God.* It is with him that man has to enter into an alliance.

This communion that man enters into with this other reality, God, made manifest in Christ (Jn 16:25–28; 14:8–11), must be lived in a human community. But this human community is not possible without man living his human identity, living what he is. That is to say, the human community is at the same time the fruit and the cause of the identity, the integrity of man. Man indeed becomes more human, more himself, because there is a community. And this humanisation, this human authenticity is made concrete, made effective only through the humanisation of the very society in which he lives. And where, therefore, man does not find his identity, where man cannot live his identity, the community cannot exist, and so the communion with God cannot be realised.

So in this light, the realisation itself of his identity as man is indispensable from his salvation, since that is what makes the communion with the Father possible and in which communion alone is found the reconciliation for man himself.

Thus every step taken in the humanisation of the environment in which man lives, is already itself within this context of the liberation of man from his situation of nonsalvation, and therefore within the order of salvation itself, a certain degree of salvation is achieved. Because this step that is taken, this act, if it is authentically human, makes the human community possible and so makes the communion with God, which is entered into through this human community, also possible.

In fact, the Christian revelation affirms that the heart of man is the principal source of sin (Mt 15:18), just as it is the heart truly converted in faith that brings about justification and salvation (Rom 10:9–10). Therefore, to reduce the causes of the situations of alienation, of nonsalvation, such as the material poverty, cultural and economic domination, political and social injustice, etc., to purely and simply exterior situations, and thus consider them only secondary, would be a betrayal of a fundamental intuition of the Message of Christ. For while Christ operated externally to better the actual and concrete conditions of the people of his time, he, above all, really preached a true conversion of man's inner-self.

How then could we see the violent and radical denunciation by Christ of these causes of sin that keep man in the nonsalvation? As Ignace Berten observes, man aspires to the kingdom, this Kingdom being the reality and gift that fulfills the expectation of man. He says:

> The message of Christ; his life, his death and his resurrection, manifests that the ultimate answer to this expectation of man is not in the political action or the political society constructed by man. Nevertheless, the violent death of Jesus condemns the political society which so unjustly condemned him to such a violent death. The death of Jesus, and because Jesus is condemned whereas he is just one, his death is the most radical contestation and denunciation of a world which kills unjustly the innocent and the just one. And by this same fact, this violent

death is an ardent appeal, which cannot be stifled, to the construction of a more just world for men to live in; and in this sense one can say that the death of Jesus is for the believer a political mobilisation.[11]

It is true that Jesus denounced sin and all its causes most radically. Yet the Christian faith is not first and foremost the denunciation of sin; it is in the first place a p r o c l a m a t i o n of salvation for man, an invitation to all men to get out of whatever situation of nonsalvation that they are in (Lk 3:4–6; 4:18–20; also Mt 4:17).

It is through this proclamation of pardon already granted, and the convocation to the building of the kingdom that the Christian faith reveals the sin in the heart of man. And it is within this framework of proclamation and construction that the denunciation of sin has any sense. To borrow once again the words of Jacques van Nieuwenhove, "There is denunciation in the framework of a convocation and of a proclamation."[12] This means that if there is a denunciation at all, it is because there is a proclamation; and hence the proclamation of the salvation is the reason for the denunciation of the situations that are the causes of this nonsalvation, and by this fact the actions within these situations themselves, if they bring man out of these situations, they have brought him salvation. This proclamation of salvation by Christ is therefore dynamic, since it calls man to an actual and effective building of the kingdom, the situation of perfect salvation. And it is this balance that the Message of Christ permits us to maintain.

CONCLUSIONS

To conclude, I would like simply to restate our thesis. What we have tried to do has been simply to see in what

16

consists the profound aspirations of man: his salvation, to which so many serious researchers have engaged themselves.

We do not pretend to have made a whole round of the problem, as that is evidently not possible in a short paper of this nature. Nevertheless, if salvation is the reason for any pastoral action in the Church, I strongly believe that one is bound, after such an analysis, to say that the pastoral action within the Church must include, in a very perceptible manner, this other dimension as part and parcel of man's salvation, and not just to direct her ministry to only the eschatological dimension of man's salvation. She must not consider the actual and concrete situations in which man lives as only secondary to the question of his salvation, and therefore only a preparation for an ulterior salvation.

Surely, one cannot suppress or even diminish the excellence and fullness of the eschatological dimension of salvation. On the contrary, as we have taken all the pains to demonstrate in this limited framework, that is indeed the completion, the totality, and plenitude of salvation towards which man is aspiring. But this plenitude will only be reached in the measure that man liberates himself, and seeks and works to liberate others from the alienated situations in which he and they exist. Thus the dichotomy by which man is divided into two, and salvation made uniquely the affair of the soul, will in my view, not be sufficient to lead man to this fullness of salvation to which he is called. Christ has announced an eschatological kingdom; he has revealed the very depths of the salvation that man is earnestly looking for.

By revealing the Father as the source of *love,* Christ has revealed the fullness of man's salvation. For, the revelation of God leads to the absolutely full revelation of man to himself. By the denunciation, through the proclamation, that he made of the social and political situations of injustices, and the poverty in which the people of his time were immersed, he had thus advocated for an unconditional engagement for a salvation of man that takes its beginning right then.

This miserable situation of man continues to exist: Man is still dominated by man, and by the conditions of alienation surrounding him; poverty and social injustices still reduce by far the majority of men to slavery. If, therefore, there is any salvation that Christ offers to man, if there is any salvation that man has to effect or to which he has to contribute, it is none other than the sum-total of all the efforts that he must make to disentangle himself from this situation, these conditions of nonsalvation. He must work to construct a human community in which it will be possible to live the communion with the *Father* that Christ has revealed as the source of reconciliation and, therefore, of *Salvation in its totality*.

Albert A. Kuuire

NOTES

1. I. Berten, "Cours de Christologie," *Lumen Vitae,* Stencilled notes for the use of students (1970–71) p. III/9.
2. *CFR Encyclopedia of Biblical Theology,* ed. J.B. Bauer, vol. 3 (London: Sheed & Ward, 1970).
3. The intervention of the wife of Nabel before David in order to obtain mercy for her husband; a deliverance of David himself from blood-guilt.
4. Cf. Also 2 Kings 16:7.
5. Amos was preaching under King Jeroboam II of the Northern Kingdom c. 783–743 B.C. Jeremiah was born c. 645. Ezekial preached among the exiled Jews in Babylon c. 593–571.
6. The Prophet Hosea, like Amos, also condemned these situations of injustice in the society of Israel at his time, although he emphasized more the religious infidelity.

7. P. Smulders, *La Vision de Teillard de Chardin,* (Paris: 1964).
8. J. B. Bauer, *Encyclopedia of Biblical Theology,* vol. 3 (London: 1970), 807–808.
9. J.H. Walgrave, *Le Salut aux Dimensions du Monde* (Paris: 1970).
10. Cf. J. B. Bauer, *Encyclopedia of Biblical Theology,* vol. 2, (London: 1970), pp. 455–470; Cf. also Lk 7:22 ff.; Mt 11:4 ff. and again Lk 4:18 ff.
11. In the course on "Christologie," *Lumen Vitae,* 17 April 1972.
12. From the course on *"Theologie, Pastorale et Développement," Lumen Vitae,* 29 February, 1972.

African Parallels for the Jewish Concept and Ritual of Blood

INTRODUCTION

"In fact, according to the Law almost everything has to be purified with blood; and if there is no shedding of blood, there is no remission. Obviously, only the copies of heavenly things can be purified in this way, and the heavenly things themselves have to be purified by a higher sort of sacrifice than this" (Heb 9:22,23).

This statement of the author of the Letter to the Hebrews, indeed the whole letter, makes so much sense to the African. This is mainly because the symbolism of "blood," "high priesthood," and "sacrifice of the Old Testament," so aptly employed by the author, finds strong parallels in the religious life of the entire black Africa.

As a matter of fact, the things that most impress and leave many questions in the mind of an African biblical student are the striking similarities between the biblical account and the African life ethos. This is so especially with the Old Testament account. The concept and ritual of blood so very important for both the Old Testament and African sacrifices is one of the areas where the similarities become even more formidable.

It is the objective of this paper to treat some of these African parallels, with the hope that more interest will be aroused in the future for further serious African contributions to the understanding of the problem of blood in the Bible in particular and the biblical message as a whole. The possibility of attaining such an objective becomes only too real when we consider the fact that the history of religion as a whole has an important role to play in the solution of the ambivalency of the use of the term "blood" in the Bible.[1] Also the presence of Africa in Israel's history during the biblical revelation[2] makes it understandable that the African traditional religions can and should contribute to the understanding of the biblical message.

Even though the material of this paper concerns mostly the Kassena-Nankana, the Mole groups of Northern Ghana and Burkina Faso and Akan in general, the employment of the phrase, "African Parallels," is by no means out of place. Despite the fact that these rituals differ a lot in different parts of Africa, there is a unifying thread that runs through all the religious practices in the continent. It is mostly in this unifying thread that are to be found the parallels between the Old Testament events and the African life and thought. The concept and ritual of blood is one of them and any serious study of it among the various ethnic groups in Africa cannot but come out with more or less the same conclusions, *res matatis mutandis*. We therefore conclude that what this paper is dealing with, is typical in the whole of Africa.

The Jewish concept of blood will be taken here to mean what the word probably stood for, situated in the Old Testament setting and later Jewish thought, as in the Letter to the Hebrews. These concepts have undoubtedly provided the basis for the New Testament understanding of blood[3] and consequently would include also the New Testament understanding of the word.

The Jewish concept of blood in its literal meaning seems to present no problems for theologians. For even if it was still a far cry from the modern biological meaning, it certainly invoked an unequivocal meaning in the Hebrew mind.[4] The blood rituals of the Old Testament also were governed by such precise and detailed prescriptions as to leave no equivocation in the mind of the biblical Jew.

However, theologians are in disagreement as to the further significance beyond the literal meaning of blood—idiomatic or symbolic meanings—which the word carries in the Old Testament and especially in the New, which derives its significance from the Old.

BIBLICAL CONCEPT OF BLOOD: A CENTURY OF RESEARCH

Finding parallels of biblical concept and ritual of blood in the African traditional religion presupposes a generally accepted notion of "blood" in the Old Testament sacrificial ritual. However, nowhere in the Old Testament is the term blood specifically defined or explained. The blood ritual was taken by the biblical Jew as a sacred divine institution, its significance taken for granted, leaving no room for questions. The whole principle laid down by divine ordinance was that "the blood is the life."[5] Rabbinical Judaism maintained more or less the same attitude later.[6]

Only in this century have attempts been made to define the biblical use of the word "blood." It may be safe to say that Professor William Milligan in his book, *The Resurrection of Our Lord*,[7] laid the foundation for the modern attempts to ascertain the biblical concept of the term. It seems fair also to say that this modern attempt owes its success to English scholars, even though two German scholars and one French[8] have also given valuable contributions. Noteworthy also is the contribution that Italian scholars have recently given, carrying forward and deepening the English contribution.[9]

In my view, Milligan stressed so much that the term "blood" in the Bible stands for both "death" and "life," two separate and independent but complementary notions, which together make a whole.[10] Unfortunately, however, subsequent scholars have each chosen one part to the exclusion of the other necessary component.

More recently, the Italian School[11] has contributed a more profound and comprehensive study on the problem. It may be fair to say that the general trend of the contributors is to equate "life" with "blood," even though a few have equated blood with both life and death or even more. Some completely new ideas have ensued from their study. Of particular interest to me is the contribution by Alberto Vanhoye,[12] for two reasons:

(a)   It calls for a serious rethinking of W. Milligan's position on the issue.
(b)   It suggests similar African concepts and ritual of blood that may help to throw some light on the dilemma.[13]

This initial paper has these two objectives in view.

A. Some African Concepts of Blood

1. GENERAL NOTION

As the Hebrews, the Africans do not have a purely abstract or biological notion of blood. However, they have a precise concept of that red liquid flowing in the bodies of human beings, birds, and animals. This significance of the term "blood," however, becomes more complex when it is employed metaphorically or symbolically and especially in ritual ceremonies.

The Kassena of Northern Ghana call blood, *gyana* or

dzana. The etymology of this word is not easy to determine with certitude. However it is not farfetched to suppose that the name *gyana (dzana)* probably comes from two words: *gya* = to hold, contain, and *na* = water. Therefore etymologically it probably means "to hold water, to be liquid," as opposed to the solid flesh in which it is found.

The Akan[14] word for blood is *mogya.* It is interesting to note the great similarity between the Kassem and Akan words, which probably come from the same root. In the Mole[15] group of languages, blood is *Ziim.*

Linguists will probably find it interesting to study the relationship between the Semitic and African roots for the world "blood." The Hebrew word *dam,* Akkadian *damu,* and the Aramaic, Ugaritic, and Arabic probably come from the same root, *dmh.*[16] The Kassena word for blood, *gyana* or *dzana* and the Akan word *mogya* could probably come from the same root, *dmh,* especially as compounds of the same word "blood" in Kassem can clearly be seen to come from the root *dmh.* (V. G. *dzam—pipalah* or *gyam-pipalah,* meaning "clotted blood," root—*dmh.)* Another interesting aspect is the *mandeo*[17] expression, *"ldma damia nisimta"*—the soul is similar to the blood, and the Mole term for blood, *ziim.* From the etymology alone of blood, it may not be easy to establish whether it stands for life or death. However the apparent similarity of the Kassem, Akan, and Mole words for blood to the Semitic root deserves a deeper study.

2. BLOOD CONSIDERED IN RELATION TO LIFE

The three classical Old Testament texts that have given rise to the discussion as to the meaning of blood in Scripture are: Genesis 9:2; Leviticus 17:10–14; Deuteronomy 12:23. The crux of the problem really is whether *nephes* (soul), *dam* (blood), and life can be equated. In Kassem and many other languages in Ghana, the same or similar reasoning as the Jews' is found.

The word *nephes* may be translated in Kassem as *gyoro* (soul). But the more appropriate word would seem to be *mimoi*, literally "nose." This means the breath of life that each individual possesses. Other languages in Ghana and Burkina Faso would translate the same word by: *nyo-voore* (Mole), "the breath of the nose." It is also so with other languages. In Ghana and Burkina Faso, therefore, there seems to exist a certain relationship among the three words: *nephes, dam,* and "life," even if this relationship is not necessarily one of simple equation.

From this conception flows the Kassena attitude to blood. In the past, to tell an African or at least a Ghanaian patient in hospital that he has no blood or sufficient blood, was to declare his case hopeless and he would surely die through fear alone. *"Noon' gyana no ti a mimoi wo ti mo na?"* "When a person's blood is finished, is his life not finished?" he would ask. Also of sacrifices, as will be seen later, the blood is considered the soul of the animal, which alone can be taken to the next world. So unless the blood of the animal is poured on the altar, the soul of the animal is not given in sacrifice. To express the idea that a woman has never given birth to a child, the Kassena would say: *"O gyana wo tu tigana ne"*—Her blood has never fallen on the ground." A few decades ago, the Kassena would never donate their blood for transfusion unless to a very close relative. This, for them, meant giving away their lives.

3. BLOOD CONSIDERED AS THE SEAT OF FEELINGS AND AS A SIGN OF THE FRAGILITY OF HUMAN NATURE

Many expressions in Ghana, especially in Kassem,

show the peoples' belief that the blood is the seat of feelings and a clear sign of the fragility of the human nature. When two children are fighting, the weaker one is usually encouraged to return the blows of the stronger one because his body too contains blood, that is, he too can feel and suffer. "*O na magem n' de mage se o de yira gyege gyana*"— "If he beats you, return the blows because his body too contains blood." Or someone who is a very hard worker is said to: "*O tunga o yira ba gyege gyana*"—"He toils as if his body had no blood." Or "*O tung o yira wi*—"He works so hard his body is dried up" (of blood). Or someone who has worked very hard to gain something, is said to have gained it at the cost of his blood. "*A li a yira gyana mo.*" Literally, "I have emptied the blood of my body for it." Therefore, for the Kassena body and blood together stand for the seat of pain, suffering, or the fragility of the human nature.[18]

4.BLOOD AND VIOLENT DEATH

The word "blood" also has a connotation of death through violence for the African. In this realm of thought, for example, the Kassena say that a candidate from the royal family, "whose hands have blood," i.e., who has committed murder in his lifetime, can never accede to the throne. This is because the "horn"—symbol of chieftaincy— abhors blood or murder. A.B. Ellis [19] mentions a similar fact in Ashanti: the king of Ashanti, Kwoffi Karikari, having been born on a Friday, made a law that no blood should be shed on that day, that is, no murder or violence should be caused on that day, in order to keep it sacred to his *Kra* i.e., his soul or guardian spirit.

More examples could be cited, and cerainly even clearer instances pertain to many ethnic groups in other parts of Africa; however, this will suffice for my purpose here.

B. Some African Blood Rituals

The African as well as the Jew of the biblical period was more at home with concrete rather than abstract things. So will his understanding of blood stand out even better in his rituals. It is especially in rituals that the African parallels so closely the biblical Jew, in the understanding of the word "blood."

1. BLOOD ESSENTIAL FOR SACRIFICE

It seems reasonable to conclude from the three classical texts of Genesis 9:4; Leviticus 17:10–14, and Deuteronomy 12:23, that blood had something definitely to do with life. Blood was considered the life of a person or any other animal.

It was considered either the same as life or life was regarded as found in blood or blood had a certain connection with life, no matter how one chose to understand the meaning of the word *nephes*. Whether this is so naturally or symbolically should not be too important for our purpose here. But we can say at least God made blood symbolise life religiously for the biblical Jew.

This then becomes the basis of other concepts of blood and any ritual having to do with blood. Atonement was therefore made possible by God because he put life in the blood or made it symbolise life in any sense.

This blood I myself have given you to perform the rite of atonement for your lives at the altar, for it is blood that atones for a life. That is why I have said to the sons of Israel: None of you nor any stranger living among you shall eat blood. If any son of Israel or any stranger living among you catches game or bird that is lawful to eat, he must pour out its blood and cover it with earth. For the life of all flesh is its blood and I have said to the sons of Israel: You must not eat the blood of any flesh, for the life of all flesh is in its blood, and anyone who eats is shall be outlawed from his people (Lv 17:11–14).

By sin man was dead, separated from God. By blood—which God made life—man, dead and separated from God, could come back to be united to God by means of the sacrificial blood.

This contact or reunion was achieved through physical and symbolic contact between God—represented by the altar—and the sinner—represented symbolically and typically in the life of the blood. The Hebrews, reasoning concretely and religiously rather than abstractly as already said, must have found that this concrete and symbolic manner of atonement suited their life conditions perfectly. To try to explain this phenomenon later, merely abstractly, is to miss the point completely.

We find exactly the same parallel concept of the significance of blood—and especially sacrificial blood—among Africans even today. Though the African cannot by any means claim such a clearly defined religious concept of blood, they do have a less clear but similar ritualistic concept of blood, especially sacrificial blood.[20]

The Kassena of Ghana and Burkina Faso avoid as much as possible the use of the word "blood" whenever possible, as this seems to be considered a sacred word and as the mention of it may suggest the violation (death), shedding of the most important creation of God (life). The word "blood" is therefore used only when it cannot be avoided.

As regards sacrificial blood, the similarities of the

two words *gyana* (blood) and *gyom* (altar) are worth noting. It would seem that *gyom* necessarily derives from and calls for *gyana*. However, the general concept of sacrificial blood is as follows: To make a sacrifice, one must invoke the name of God, immolate the victim so that the blood that they call the soul of the animal, or at least the element that releases the soul of the animal, which soul is connected with the life of the animal, may flow unto the altar. Then the soul[21] *(gyoro)* of the animal is accepted by God for the ancestors.

In many parts of Africa, therefore, the sacrificial blood, just as among the Hebrews, is considered as life or giving life. Because of this, the immolation of the victim is essential for any bloody sacrifice. This is so even in all cases where the word "pour" is used to designate sacrifice as the Akkadian word *naqu* (pour) or the Hittite word *sipand*.[22] In Ghana and Upper Volta, the Kassena and Mole-root languages use the word "pour" to designate sacrifice: *Ka bagre* (Mole-root languages), *"lo na"*—"pour water" or *"Kaane gyom"*—"pour on the altar," which both mean to make a sacrifice.

However, it would be completely false to conclude from this that blood was not essential for sacrifice. Besides the blood poured on the altar, the rest of the blood is collected and cooked with the liver (considered the seat of the blood—life), and part of this meal is offered on the altar before being participated by the worshipers. On the contrary, because blood is considered life, it is very repulsive to talk of it, as that would give the impression of brutality, namely, taking life violently. The word "blood" is therefore veiled in the word "water," which is the flour water *munnah* (Kassem) or *minhah* (Hebrew), which must always precede every bloody sacrifice. The Kassena name for "blood" even includes "water" (*Gyana*—hold water, be liquid).

Therefore in making a bloody sacrifice in Africa, it is essential that the blood of the victim touch or flow unto the altar. If the victim is a bird, some feathers are plucked and placed or stuck to the blood on the altar. If an animal, some hair is sometimes also pulled and stuck to the blood on the altar.[23] This symbolises the offering of the whole victim. In other words, the blood, with or without the feathers, represents the totality of the life of the victim.

Another interesting phenomenon in Africa is the eating of blood. Precisely because the blood is considered life, the African may eat part of the blood that has been cooked and offered together with the liver on the altar. However it is also worth noting that in the past many Africans practically never killed any animal just for the sake of the meat. The animal nearly always had to be sacrificed before the meat could be eaten. In this case the blood was almost invariably shed before (cf. Gn 9:4; Lv 17:10–14; Dt 12:23).

In this regard another ritual is worth mentioning: upon the death of a man, a sheep is usually killed by striking or dashing its head three times on the ground. *"Ne fera"* it is called. The dead person is to take this animal with him to the next world to start a new life. Only the undertaker in this case may eat the meat. Anyone else who touches it will die, so it is believed. This is probably because of the blood in the meat, as in some areas the practice is now to slaughter the animal for the blood to flow so that other people may participate in the meat.

Another sign of the connection of life with blood is that among certain tribes in Africa, whenever one's *"juju,"* i.e., fetish or magic, requires a human sacrifice where it is not possible to procure a human victim, one is permitted to cut one's own finger for the blood to flow into the altar. This is accepted as human sacrifice because the human blood is human life.

Finally another important factor, which should have been mentioned earlier, is the interesting similarity in the Moshi names for both blood and life: The Moshis of Upper Volta call blood, *ziim* and life, *viim*. Is this merely a coincidence?

2. BLOOD PACTS

The concept of blood-life relationship seems to be clearly manifested in the "blood pact" ritual in many parts of Africa. In these rites, bosom friends can become "blood brothers." They do this by cutting parts of their bodies (usually arms) to let blood flow and then sucking each other's blood in turn, or they exchange each other's blood and rub it into their own blood or any similar practice varying according to the various places. After this they are considered "blood brothers." In other words the same life now flows through them and they are one.

Among the Kassena both of Northern Ghana and Burkina Faso, this ritual was also in force in the past but is now defunct. What continued for some time was the blood pact between husbands and wives. When a man and his wife loved each other to the utmost, each one secretly cut his arm. They sucked each other's blood and from that moment, they considered themselves absolutely one. They had to love each other to the end, and absolutely no evil work could be indulged in by either of them against the other. They were not even permitted to listen to any evil said against their partner.

More than that, they believed that when one died, the other must follow immediately, (a day or two after, or as the funeral was being performed) as there was nothing again worth living for in life.[24] This ritual is called: *nyo kwora* i.e., the drinking of the horn. The mention of the word "blood" is veiled under the name of "horn" or *zu gyaro,* which is very close to "to enter blood."

Another blood pact among the Kassena is the sealing of the reconciliation with a newly elected chief, called *Pe seem.* At the death of a chief among the Kassena, all sons and nephews contest for the chieftaincy out of right and duty. Sometimes after the lawful candidate has been elected, the rest must go to be reconciled with the chief.

This reconciliation is sealed by eating together the liver of the cow sacrificed to the *kwora* (horn), symbol of chieftaincy. The liver, considered the seat of blood, part of which is sacrificed to the horn, is then shared by all former contestants and the chief. Anyone who goes against the chief afterwards or breaks the pact, will surely be killed by the horn, so they believe.

3. BLOOD FOR PURIFICATION

We can say the blood-life connotation represented in the sacrificial blood has been extended to the capacity of the blood to purify.[25] The best parallels of the biblical blood-ritual purifications[26] are to be found especially among the Ashantis and the other Akan groups of Ghana.

The "Odwira" or "Odwira-tuo" festival is an annual festival of purification celebrated for the annual worship of the great tutelary gods of the nation, the sanctification of the stools and their holders, and for the purification of the people from their transgressions of the passing year. Besides many other purificatory rites, a sheep is sacrificed in the stool house and its blood poured on each stool. The door-posts are also smeared with sacrificial blood, and both the king and the worshipers receive due sanctification in the blood of the sacrificial lamb, the forehead of each of them being sealed with three vertical strokes with the central fingers of the right hand of the priest, dipped in the blood of the sacrificial lamb. A similar rite is done also in the mausoleum of the dead kings.[27]

The Kassena too have ritual purifications that avoid the mention of the word "blood" for reasons already mentioned. However, their beliefs in the vengeance incumbent on posterity for blood that was shed in a family in a way parallels the Jewish belief in the biblical texts. When a Kassena kills a person, he must undergo a certain purification; otherwise, they believe the soul of the murdered will always haunt him, requesting his death in revenge. The ritual is called *zu na*—"to enter water, be purified" or *sang kyao* or *sang dogha*. With hens, goats, and sheep, he goes to the person in charge of the purification rites. He is isolated for nine days during which bloody sacrifices are made, his head is shaved, and water poured over it for purification. During this time, the soul of the murdered comes every night to torment the murderer, demanding vengeance.[28] This soul is finally driven away forever by the priest and the ritual.

Among the Kassena also, when a person dies, leaving grand- and great-grandchildren, at his funeral, all the grand- and great-grandchildren must have their cheeks marked with red earth, charcoal, and ashes respectively. This rite is called *tang gyunu*. We see here again the word *gyunu* replacing *gyana* (blood), because of its sacredness. This rite has a double meaning. It shows that the grandchildren, great-grandchildren, etc., all have the same blood (life) as the dead person.

They are his blood. Second, it serves to ward off evil. If the dead person is a bad man and wants to catch his grandchildren to carry his things to the next world (because they play with him), then these grandchildren are protected by the sign of his own blood.

Finally, one very notable blood ritual among the Kassena and among other African tribes, which shows an ambivalent association of blood to both life and death, is called *Pe gyana,* i.e., to collect blood violently shed on the land.

When the land (Mother Earth) has been desecrated by having blood (human) shed on her through murder, accidents, or other serious crimes, then she must be purified by a bloody sacrifice of a sheep or cow on the spot where the shedding of the blood was supposed to have taken place.[29] This is because they believe that blood violently shed on the land pollutes or desecrates it and it will never yield good crops. Moreover, similar accidents will continue to occur on the same spot unless the land is purified by "collecting" the spilt blood.[30] The name of the ritual itself suggests that blood is identified with death, because what is collected (the blood violently shed) is called "blood." On the other hand, the ritual itself suggests that blood brings life. For it is the blood of an animal offered in sacrifice that purifies the land and returns it to a productive state (life).

The same name and ritual prevails when human blood is violently shed on the land, even though not to the point of death. This is true also in the case of a woman delivering a child in her parents' house rather than her husband's. In this case, even though the action is not considered violent, the place is considered a foreign land and therefore renders the action legally or customarily wrong. It seems to be a pretext of compensating for the labour of the parents-in-law.

C. The Letter to the Hebrews and the African Concept

The key to the understanding of the use of the word "blood" in Scripture seems to be in the Epistle to the Hebrews. If this is the case, a better understanding of sacrifices and blood ritual in Africa may help to throw light on the use of blood in Scripture.

The unknown author of Hebrews "ΠΡΟΣ ΕΒΡΑΙΟΥΣ" seems to be addressing himself to a particular local group or circle, whose identity, like that of the author, is not known today. His aim seems to have been to correct and exhort his audience faced with a critical situation in their Christian faith. This critical situation was a practical failure to be loyal to the principle that Christianity is the absolute religion. The author argues purely from the symbolism of "blood," "high-priesthood," and sacrifice of the Old Testament. Even though he mentions other ritual sacrifices of the Old Testament, his principal reference is to the Tabernacle sacrifices and not to those of the Temple.

Even here, he is heavily influenced by the annual atonement-day ritual of the Tabernacle, when the high priest entered once a year into the Holy of Holies with the blood of animals and smeared the "ιλαστ≥ηριον" (the cover of the ark) with the blood (Lv 16). Not even the scapegoat ritual is mentioned by the author. To illustrate his point, the author uses the Pentateuch texts and the Psalter. He uses particularly the LXX, preferring the Codex Alexandrinus.

The reason why the author uses the priesthood, blood, and sacrifice of Christ to illustrate his point is partly because of his concept of religion. For him there is no religion without a priest and worship. He therefore shows that only the Christian faith fulfills the conditions of real religion.

The author is primarily influenced by a religious philosophy of his own among the New Testament writers. However, the philosophical element in his view of the world and God is fundamentally Platonic. He reasons somewhat like Philo and the author of the Book of Wisdom, namely, that the phenomenal is but an imperfect, shadowy transcript of what is eternal and real. He differs from Philo, however, in being ritualistic rather than abstract. The author's concept of religion as devotion or worship helps to explain why he represents Jesus after his death as being raised from the dead, but as passing through the heavens into the inner Presence or Sanctuary of God with the sacrifice of his blood (Heb 4:14; 9:11 ff).

The heavenly sphere of Jesus is so closely linked with his previous existence on earth, under the category of sacrifice, that the author could not suggest an experience like the Resurrection, which would not have tallied with this idea of continuity.[31]

Myles M. Bourke[32] comments that the author of Hebrews shares the view found in Romans 1:3 ff. that so far as his human nature is concerned, Jesus became Son of God in the fullest sense at his Resurrection; until then, he existed in that condition Paul calls "the likeness of sinful flesh" (Rom 8:3; cf. Heb 5:7; 10:20). For this reason, Bourke concludes that the blessing in 13:20–21 contains the only explicit reference in Hebrews to the Resurrection, but it is always presupposed when Jesus' exaltation is mentioned.

With all this strong Old Testament background of the author of Hebrews in view, what are the bases for the comparison of the Letter with the pagan sacrificial rituals? First of all, the relationship between the Letter to the Hebrews and the pagan rituals as proposed by this work is to be considered an indirect one, through the Old Testament.

Some scholars see a probable influence of the sacrificial rituals of the ancient Near East, especially those of Israel's neighbours, on the Israelite cultus, including the Levitical sacrificial cultus.[33] Therefore, at least indirectly, one can say that the pagan rituals probably had an influence on the Letter to the Hebrews. Also very recently, J. Swetnam in his book, *Jesus and Isaac,* argues very convincingly through the interpretation of literary texts, that "the Aqedah not only as it existed in Genesis 22 but also as it existed in Jewish tradition influenced the Epistle: the efficacy of Jesus' sacrifice as against Isaac's, Jesus' offering himself to die, the role of the shedding of blood in the expiation of sins, the importance of spiritual descent from Abraham—all these factors point in this direction."[34]

This present paper therefore, taking off from this point of view, maintains that since the pagan rituals probably influenced the Aqedah, they probably also, but indirectly through the Aqedah, influenced the Lettter to the Hebrews. This would not be a novelty, for even Myles M. Bourke comments in the JBC on Hebrews 1:5–13, that these verses probably reflect an enthronement hymn similar to Philippians 2:9–11 and Timothy 3:16, in which the stages of Jesus' exaltation are given in the order corresponding to that of ancient Near Eastern (especially Egypt) enthronement ceremonies (cf. J. Jeremias, Die Briefe an Timotheus und Titus (Göttingen: NTD, 1965), 4, 22–24).

The three stages are:

(1) the elevation of the new king to divine status;
(2) his presentation to the gods of the pantheon;
(3) his enthronement and reception of kingly power.

With the modification demanded by a monotheistic religion (Jesus is not presented to the gods but to angels), the sequence can be seen in these verses:

(1) Jesus' elevation to the rank of Son of God, whom angels must adore (5–6);

(2) the proclamation of everlasting lordship (7–12);
(3) the enthronement (13).[35]

Second, the author of Hebrews' strong use of the symbolisms of "blood," "priesthood," and sacrifice find equally strong parallels in the pagan world, especially Africa. J. Moffatt states in his critical and exegetical commentary on the Epistle to the Hebrews, referred to above, that "symbolism alters as the ages pass. The picture-language in which one age expresses its mental or religious conceptions often ceases to be intelligible or attractive to later generations, because the civic, ritual or economic conditions of life which had originally suggested it have disappeared or changed their form."

This well-known principle applies especially to the language of religion, and it is one reason why some of the arguments in "ΠΡΟΣ ΕΒΡΑΙΟΥΣ" are so difficult to follow the exegetical methods that the author took over from the Alexandrian School are not ours. Besides, historical criticism has rendered it hard for us moderns to appreciate the naive use of the Old Testament that prevails in some selections of "ΠΡΟΣ ΕΒΡΑΙΟΥΣ·" But above all, the sacrificial analogies are a stumbling block, for we have nothing to correspond to what an ancient understood by a "priest" and "sacrifice."[36]

True to this principle, the Epistle to the Hebrews was appealing to the Church of North Africa and of particular interest to the Alexandrian Church, because they had everything to correspond to what an ancient understood by a "priest" and sacrifice.[37] And true also to the same principle, the Epistle is appealing to the Africans even today, because they have similar sacrificial analogies to correspond to what an ancient or the author of the Epistle understood by "priest" and sacrifice.

A. Vanhoye, a well-known authority on the Letter to the Hebrews, clearly stresses the Christian understanding of the symbolisms employed by the author. Vanhoye's works, especially *"Mundatio per Sanguinem* (Heb 9,22,23)" and *"Il Sangue di Cristo nell 'Epistola agli Ebrei,"* are very pertinent for the African understanding.[38] J. Swetnam has also clarified some of these issues discussed by Vanhoye, especially in *"Mundatio per Sanguinem."*[39]

This paper, therefore, basing itself on these works, finds the comparisons of the Letter to the Hebrews with the pagan rituals, especially those of Africa today, not out of place.

From both the Letter to the Hebrews and the African concept and ritual of blood, therefore, there seems to be no reason why blood in Scripture cannot stand for both life and death. The author of the Epistle to the Hebrews, especially in Chapter 9:23-10:23, speaks so clearly and convincingly that we can only conclude that the Old Testament concept and ritual of blood was merely a symbol, a type to be fulfilled in Christ, the Reality. Therefore what in the natural state may seem contradictory or ambivalent does not necessarily fail to symbolise and presage a spiritual reality. Only the blood of Christ can truly be said to be life. The blood of animals and man symbolised and typified this reality. The shedding of blood of man and animals also symbolised and typified the death of Christ. But then this is religiously the making of God, especially in the Old Testament.

The same idea has been clearly stated, and the conclusion that blood stands for both death and life has been implied by Professor William Milligan[40] in his exposition of the Epistle to the Hebrews. If, as he argues, the slaughtering of the animal and the sprinkling of the blood on the great day of Atonement each occupied a necessary place, and expressed an idea to a certain extent independent of—although at the same time closely related to—that of the other, then consequently it is not difficult to understand why the term "blood" could stand both for death and life.

The whole problem in my opinion should therefore be not whether the term "blood" in Scripture stands for death or life, but when and how does it stand for death and when and how, for life.

CONCLUSIONS

1. From the foregoing, it would seem that the African concept and ritual of blood connotes both death and life. These are two different but related states of a fragile human nature, which this same name "blood" can also stand for. My investigation, held among the Kassena-Nankana of Northern Ghana and some Akans, and the Kassena and Moshis of Burkina Faso, seems to confirm this. Even though this study is limited to a very small geographical area of Africa, it is my strong belief that studies of other areas of Africa will not fail to come up with similar or even clearer findings. For the subject matter touches on something common to all parts of Africa, namely sacrifices.

2. In my study of the various works on the use of the term "blood," in Scripture and the African concept and ritual of the same blood, I have come to conclude that the African concept and rituals parallel many aspects of the use of the word in Scripture. This is by no means to put them on the same level. The scriptural concept has its particularity and Jewish characteristic. It is a specific revelation by God to a specific people—the Jewish na-

tion—at specific moments of salvation history. As such it is unique.

On the other hand, the African concept is less clear, full of many superstitions, and its origin not easy to determine. However, these parallels do suggest some influences between these various groups and the Hebrew peoples.

The African concept and ritual of blood is only but one of many areas where there exist parallels between his traditional religion and culture and those of the Old Testament Hebrew and other Semitic peoples.[41] Such areas include: the reasoning and talking in images and symbols and sacrifices in general, just to mention a few.

It is my belief that whatever reasons may be offered for these African parallel concepts and ritual of blood, there must have been a historical contact between the Semites, including the Hebrews, and the Africans where there were reciprocal influences of cultures and religions or both were influenced by a parent stock or both. Similar ideas have been expressed by quite a few writers of migrations and distributions in Africa. Migeod[42] writes that there has been rather a tendency to ascribe to Egypt an undue influence, though it is not denied it was great. Where this is done he maintains, other former important influences, such as the Hebrew one, have been overlooked.

The point is that a better understanding of sacrifices and blood rituals in Africa may help to throw light on the use of blood in Scripture.

3. It becomes apparent too that the African concept and ritual of blood not only could help for the understanding of the use of the term "blood" in Scripture but also that the African has a solid foundation to rise to the understanding and acceptance of the salvation in Jesus Christ, especially as presented by the author of the Letter to the Hebrews.

If there is no purification except through the shedding of blood, then the African is in better stead to understand that his ritual of purification with blood—*Pe gyana, Odwira* purifications, etc., were only a dream, a far-cry, a premonition of the Cross of Christ, which is the reality, purifying the blood of man shed by the devil and our first parents. A careful treatise of this aspect would be a good summary of salvation history for the African.

4. Finally the African blood rituals, but especially the blood pacts, are such fertile grounds for the understanding and full participation of the sacramental life of the Church, most especially, the Holy Eucharist. If sucking each other's blood to become blood-brothers can have a profound influence in the life of the African, how much more profound an effect the death of Christ, the sacraments of the Church, and especially the drinking of the Blood of Christ, have on the Christian life of the African.

By his death, Resurrection, and his sacraments, Christ has bled for us to suck so as to be his brothers. The only thing left for us to complete the ritual is to bleed also our blood for Christ, which will consist in our carrying our daily crosses after him until the end.

Joseph W. Apuri

NOTES

1. F. Vattioni, ed. *"Sangue: Vita o Morte Nella Bibbia?" Sangue e Antropologia Biblica* (Rome: 1980), p. 367.
2. R.A. Bennett, Jr., "Africa and the Biblical Period," *Harvard Theological Review* 64 (1971): 484–485.
3. F. Vattioni, *Sangue,* p. 367.
4. L. Morris, "The Biblical Use of the Term 'Blood,' " *J.T.S.* 6 (1955): 77.
5. Gn 9:4; Lv 17:10–12; Dt 12:23. See also V. Talor, *Jesus and His Sacrifice* (London: 1937), p. 49.
6. *Jewish Encyclopedia,* X 628; G.F. More; article on "Sacrifice,"

Encycl. Biblica, col. 4226.

7. W. Milligan, *The Resurrection of Our Lord* (London: 1881).
8. F. Vattioni, *Sangue,* p. 369.
9. Ibid.
10. W. Milligan, *The Resurrection,* especially pp. 135, 264.
11. F. Vattioni, *Sangue.*
12. A. Vanhoye, "Il Sangue di Christo nell'Epistola agli Ebrei," in F. Vattioni, *Sangue,* pp. 819–829.
13. See F. Vattioni, *Sangue,* p. 367.
14. Akan is the common name given to all the languages spoken in Southern Ghana and Ashanti, with the exception of a few.
15. Mole is the root of some main languages spoken in Northern Ghana and part of Upper Volta (Moshi).
16. See F. Vattioni, *Sangue,* p. 372.
17. Ibid., p. 373.
18. See A. Vanhoye, "Il Sangue," p. 821.
19. A.B. Ellis, *The Tshui-Speaking Peoples of the Gold Coast of West Africa* (London: 1887), p. 156.
20. A practical field work was conducted in Ouagadougou, Po, and Kyakane in the Upper Volta and the following is from this field work. So also J.B. Danquah, *The Gold Coast Akan* (London: 1945), who on page 16 says, "The principal element of sacrifice is the blood of the clean or precious animal which is poured out."
21. This "soul" seems to have a slightly different meaning from the European soul. Even inanimate things seem to have souls in this case. See A.B. Ellis *Tshui-Speaking Peoples,* p. 149ff.
22. D.J. McCarthy, *Symbolism of Blood and Sacrifice," JBL* 88 (1969): 167.
23. See A.V. Cardinall, *The Natives of the Northern Territories of the Gold Coast: Their Customs, Religion, and Folklore* pp. 23, 32, 33; F.A. Arinze, *Sacrifice in Ibo Religion* (Ibadane: 1970), p. 98; R.S. Rattray, *Ashanti* (New York: 1923), pp. 96–97, 112; T.E. Bowdich, *Mission from Cape Coast to Ashanti* (London: 1819), pp. 279ff.; J. Goody, *Death, Property and Ancestors* (Stanford: 1962), pp. 118–120.
24. The Kassena interviewed in Po, Burkina Faso, say that there is a special ritual to save the life of the second partner but even after such a second ritual has been performed, he or she always remained somewhat subhuman in his or her capacity for reasoning, until he or she eventually died.
25. A.M. Stebbs, pp. 13,14.
26. The Passover Ritual: (Ex 12:1–13); Sin and guilt-offerings: (Lv 4:6), and Day of Atonement: (Ex 30:10).
27. J.B. Danquah, *Akan Laws and Customs and the Akim Abuarwa*

Constitution (London: 1928), pp. 128–140; see also A.B. Ellis, *Tshui,* pp. 228ff.; R. S. Rattray, *Ashanti,* p. 134; E.L.R. Meyerowitz, *The Sacred State of the Akan* (London: 1951), pp. 17ff.

28. Gn 9:4–7; Dt 19:11–13.

29. A.W. Cardinall, *Op Cit.,* p. 60.

30. Compare this with Nm 35:33; Ps 106:38.

31. For all this, see J. Moffatt, *A Critical and Exegetical Commentary on the Epistle to the Hebrews* (ICC) (Edinburgh: 1979), pp. XIIIff, especially pp. XXXVIII and XLV.

32. R.E. Brown, S. S., J.A. Fitzmeyer, R.E. Murphy, eds. Op. Cit., pp. 384, 402–403.

33. See works of Pedersen, Spiegel, Rosenberg, and the Ras Shamra Texts and the particular work of G.B. Gray, *Sacrifice in the Old Testament.*

34. J. Swetnam, *Jesus and Isaac.* See especially pp. 83ff.; 119ff. and 122ff.

35. R.E. Brown, S.S., J.A. Fitzmeyer, R.E. Murphy, eds., Op. Cit., p. 384 Col. 2, n. 12.

36. J. Moffatt, *Exegetical Commentary,* p. XIVI.

37. Ibid.

38. See A. Vanhoye, "Mundatio per Sanguinem" (Heb 9:22–23) VD 44 (1966): 177–182, and "Il Sangue di Cristo Nell' Epistola agli Ebrei," in F. Vattioni, ed., *Sangue e Antropologia Biblica,* 1981, pp. 819–829.

39. See J. Swetnam, S.J. *Jesus and Isaac,* especially pp. 186ff.

40. W. Milligan, *The Resurrection,* pp. 135ff. and note 53 on p. 135, pp. 263ff.

41. I would refer readers to the works of: J.J. Williams, *Hebrews of West Africa,* (New York: 1930); T.E. Bowdich, "An Essay on the Superstitions, Customs, and Arts, Common to the Ancient Egyptians, Abyssianians, and Ashantees," (monograph) (Paris: 1821); E.L.R. Meyerowitz, *The Sacred State of the Akan* (London: 1958), *The Akan Divine Kingship and Its Prototype in Ancient Egypt* (London: 1961); P.M. Renju, "African Traditional Religion and Old Testament: Continuity of Discontinuity?" *Christianisme et identité Africaine* (Kinshasa: 1978); K.A. Dickson, "Continuity and Discontinuity Between the Old Testament and African Life Thought,": *Bulletin of African Theology* Vol. 1. no. 2. (1979): 179–193. Also my own unpublished work.

42. F.R.H. Migeod, *The Languages of West Africa* (London: 1911), especially pp. 35ff.

The Catholic Church in West Africa: Historico-Pastoral Perspectives

After several renewed efforts by various missionaries to implant the Catholic faith in Africa, there developed a steady growth both in numbers and quality in some countries. Such lucky countries in which the Church succeeded to be implanted have started one after the other to celebrate the centenary of her foundation. All over Africa, especially south of the Sahara, one gets the impression that the Catholic Church (as well as the other Christian Churches) have come to stay, despite the vicissitudes and fluctuations of African political history.

This impression should not, however, lead us to a false complacency that can easily cause a certain blindness to the challenges of the future and even certain demands of the present. In this contribution, it is not my intention to give a triumphalistic history and account of the achievements of the Catholic Church but rather to stimulate some reflection on the challenges of the present and the future of the Church in Africa. It is my contention that every growth reaches a critical point at which the right response has to be made or otherwise it becomes a lost opportunity. Optimists like Father Walbert Buehlmann, and others who think like him, believe that now is the hour for the expansion and glory of the Third Church, which he describes as the Church of the Third World.

According to Father Walbert Buehlmann, the first millennium was the era of the Church of the East, the second millennium was the era of the Church of the West, and now the third millennium, which will soon begin, will be the era of the Church of the South, which covers in great part the Third World countries: Africa, Latin America, and others.[1] Without dismissing such optimism, we have to say that it will all depend on how the challenges of the present and the future will be met by the young Church in such developing countries. The main aim of this paper is to show the need to review the history of the Church, her mode of being implanted in our young nations with their multiple problems, and a revision of the strategy used as far as the priorities are concerned.

In the first part, we shall be content with certain generalities that statistics provide. In this way we hope to depict the phenomenon of the established Church: her high points, her problems and challenges, and her hope for the future. In these reflections our main point of reference is Ghana whose successes and failures will be generalised. I consider this legitimate because of a certain common background that permits such a generalisation. Throughout this geographic region of Africa, there is a certain common pattern of socio-political development in which the same problems can be identified.

Thus the colonial and missionary era, the struggle for independence, the building up of nationalism, the struggle for social, economic, and political stability, and the growth of the post-independence Church, can all be considered as stages of the common pattern of development.

1. BRIEF HISTORICAL AND STATISTICAL DATA

The Church in West Africa from Senegal to Niger has been the fruit of the renewed and determined missionary efforts of mid-nineteenth century. All along West Africa, we find a network of churches surviving the competing faith of Islam. The Catholic Church, which in some countries was a late-comer, is entering or has already entered her centenary. For instance Ghana has celebrated her centenary in 1980, which event was crowned by the visit of Pope John-Paul II in May of the same year.

It was from 1880 onwards that the Catholic Church found greater tolerance and witnessed the founding of new missionary societies prepared for more organised and stable missions in Africa. In this connection the White Fathers, founded by Cardinal Lavigerie in 1868, the Society of African Missions, the Holy Ghost Fathers, and the Society of the Divine Word should be mentioned.

In 1880 Fathers Auguste Moreau and Eugene Murat arrived in Elmina to reestablish the Catholic faith there. The number of baptised Catholics rose steadily from year to year and from one region to the other, despite the death toll of many missionaries.

In 1901 Monsignor Maximillian Albert, S.M.A., was consecrated the first Bishop of the Gold Coast. The Apostolic Prefecture of the Gold Coast was entrusted to the Society of African Missions (S.M.A.). Soon afterwards other missionary societies of both men and women arrived from different backgrounds and joined hands in the work of evangelisation. In 1906 three White Fathers, Father

Chollet, Father Morin, and Brother Eugene arrived in Navrongo from Ouagadougou through a roundabout route via Wa on the 23rd of April and settled down there to begin the work of evangelisation in the north.

It is beyond my scope to give the details of the origins of the Catholic Church in the various countries. Each of the countries where the Church exists today has its own peculiar and interesting history, which cannot be adequately handled in a paper like this one. Each of the African countries would have to write its own history of origins, with the proper names and dates connected with the foundation of the Church there.

However, the one thing that is common to all is the pattern of missionary work in founding the Church. In various areas the founding missionaries used the same methods in their work of evangelisation: first primary education, health care, teaching technical skills, and then catechetical instruction. What is evident in this method is the predominance of the human development of the people being evangelised.

From another point of view, we can say that the human development of the people was a natural consequence of the conversion resulting from the missionary activity. From the point of view of the human development of the people, we can consider it a remarkable achievement of the Church to have produced educated men who later became prominent personalities in the political and social development of their countries. Missionary work was, therefore, not just in function of direct conversions but opened up all kinds of potentialities for the future of Africa. Whether all this can be considered positive depends on how we view the priorities of the mission of the Church.

THE CATHOLIC CHURCH IN FIGURES: A BIRD'S-EYE VIEW OF GROWTH

From Senegal to Niger, we can review the external growth of the Catholic Church through the following figures:

COUNTRY	POPULATION	CATHOLICS	PERCENTAGE
Cameroon	6,400,000	1,633,000	29%
Gambia	520,000	11,530	2.2%
Ghana	9,870,000	1,218,338	11.9%
Guinea	4,420,000	42,376	0.9%
Ivory Coast	4,890,000	617,300	12%
Nigeria	102,930,000	4,195,490	6.8%
Senegal	4,140,000	191,590	4.6%
Sierra Leone	3,110,000	47,010	1.5%
Togo	2,220,000	457,400	20%
Upper Volta	6,030,000	404,410	7%
Niger	4,600,000	13,000	0.3%
TOTAL	109,130,000	8,832,444	8.7%

The total population of Africa was 391,178,000 with a total Catholic population of 46,292,000, in 1976. According to these figures the Catholic population represented then an average of 11.8% of the total population of Africa.[2]

TABLES SHOWING THE INCREASE OF CATHO-LICS FROM 1900-1977

Year	Number of Native Priests	Number of Catholics	Ecclesiastical Division
1900	—	2,378.824	47
1949	1,080	14,848,622	—
1959	2,072	—	—
1966	—	31,781,816	318
1969	2,623	—	—
1972	4,200	41,746,000	356
1977	—	46,292,000	371

These figures have a great significance when they are placed in the history of the Church in the continent as a whole. Two great decades are outstanding and attract the attention of the keen observer, and they are the period between 1952 and 1972. These decades show a remarkable external growth of the Catholic Church in the context of the general development out of the continent. The first decade, 1952-1962, marks the era of political independence and decolonisation. During this period the Catholic Church not only survived but proved that she came to stay in Africa.

Despite the upheavals of decolonisation, the Church was accepted as part and parcel of the heritage of the young nations, a distinct reality from the colonial powers of the West. The second significant decade, 1962–1972, witnessed intensive Africanisation in terms of local clergy and bishops. The following testimony of one Lutheran bishop of Bukoba in Tanzania describes the remarkable progress of the Catholic Church in Africa.

"The story of the development of the Roman Catholic Church, its priesthood in Africa in this century, is astonishing; one of the wonders of the dramatic history of world missions. . . . The spread of the Church was guided by a global strategy. Strategy and planning, not improvisation, is the strong impression given by this development."[3]

In global terms such progress in the external and visible implantation of the Church within one century is indeed impressive and monumental, considering the many and varied problems that went along with the spread of the faith. Furthermore, the second decade, 1962–1972, witnessed the Second Vatican Council with its great and unprecedented programmes of renewal in all aspects of the Church—liturgical, ecumenical, pastoral, theological, missionary, etc. In short this was the decade of radical reforms in the Catholic Church, which are still being implemented everywhere.

In the wake of the renewal of Vatican II, the African Church is called upon to face the challenges and responsibilities of the local Church. In this awareness, everywhere attempts are being made to establish the local Church with the transfer of Church leadership to the native clergy.

Pessimistic obervers are suspicious of this trend of events and are worried about the future of the Church in the hands of the local clergy. But one thing is undeniable, and it is the new vitality and potentialities of the Church in the young nations. The fact that such new potentialities can be abused is not new in the history of the Church. It is now imperative that missionaries, whatever their identity and field of specialisation, should accept the idea and identity of the local Church and seek to collaborate with the local ordinaries in the building up of the local Church and with concerted effort tackle the emerging problems of the society in which they live. The spirit of collaboration and the recognition of the existence of the local Church should be the criterion for the organisation of any missionary activity. In the words of Father Waly Neven, this spirit can be summarised as follows:

"From being independent founders of Churches, they (the missionaries) have to become servants of the local Church; from being people in authority, they have to become men of dialogue, listeners and willy-nilly, even men of obedience."[4] This spirit of collaboration will inevitably modify the identity and the image of the missionary in Africa.

3. AN URGENT CALL FOR CONSOLIDATION OF THE AFRICAN CHURCH

The data given above show the external growth of the Church in West Africa. Some historians are more inclined to enumerate the achievements of the established Church in the areas of education, health care, and socioeconomic developments. There is a lot to say about these areas of human development, which are part and parcel of the presence of the Church in Africa and indeed a witness to her interior life of charity to the world. Indeed we must acknowledge the fact that the history of West Africa cannot be written without including the achievements of the Church and her impact on human development.

However, instead of dwelling on the laurels of the Church of yesterday, we should look forward into the future and in the light of the future discern the tasks of the local Church today. Such discernment is indeed the main purpose of this paper. Today I see the work of consolidating the Church in West Africa as the most urgent priority. All the efforts of the Church must converge towards this goal.

In the past century, this work of consolidating was not possible because of the many and varied problems: linguistic, cultural, educational, and the harsh climatic conditions in which the missionaries had to work. The fact that the Church survived and expanded externally shows the divine power behind and within it. This urgent task of consolidation embraces the following priority elements: conversion, a renewed and effective catechesis, and appropriate liturgy and active participation in sacramental life, the promotion of Christian marriage and Christian families, and an effective Christian witness in public life.

i. Conversion demands the radical change of mind and heart necessary for accepting the gospel and living it out in practice, even at the cost of one's own life. It is not a matter of mere allegiance to the institutions of the Church for the many social and human advantages that one can get from them. In the past many factors concurred to lead individuals and whole tribes to the Church but which might be seen today as humanitarian and paternalistic. The demands of conversion are radical and call for a personal confrontation with the major issues of life. For such a decisive option in one's life-direction, there must be new and basic attitudes by which the whole person is engaged and behaves accordingly. The radical demands of conversion may mean in practical terms less in numbers but better in quality. Only true and thorough conversion will guarantee the future of the Church. In this light we should not base our prospects of the African Church on statistics but on the quality of the conversions. This is the only way to avoid serious crisis in the future.

ii. An effective catechesis must be seen as an indispensable instrument for conversion. In order to make it effective, we have to revise it seriously according to the demands of inculturation. Indeed, one of the greatest problems facing the local Church, which as such may be considered general, is how to cope with the mass instruction of catechumens and neophytes.

We have to become very inventive to make our catechesis really an effective instrument of conversion. This means that from catechesis we should move to an effective catechumenate that is a kind of spiritual noviciate for the future converts. In the words of Adrian Hastings, the catechumenate is the time

> when one brings the future convert into touch with the Church, presenting the Church to him, making him realise his dissatisfaction with his present non-ecclesial state. It must advance from what is positive in his existing beliefs and must work through them, showing the inadequacies of the non-Christian state. . . . It is the making of contact, the insertion of an idea of faith in Christ and membership of the Church that may alone provide an answer to the troubles and question-marks of life, the plan that God himself has given to man, the way of escape from haunting fears of death and quarrels and sorcery.[5]

In the light of all this reflection, the catechumenate should become one of the top priorities of the local Church. It is a sign of great hope for the future that today catechetical centres are springing up in different countries. To invest in such centres is very urgent for our local Churches.

iii. Liturgy and an Active Participation in Sacramental Life. The Christian Life of the local Church is built up and sustained by the liturgy and the sacraments.

Baptism is the initiation into the eucharistic community. With the renewal of music and art/symbols must come about an appropriate liturgy as the genuine expression of faith and life. But it is a very painful fact that in many areas of West Africa, a very great number of our Christians are practically deprived of the frequent and effective participation in the sacramental life of the Church, especially the Eucharist. The causes for such excommunication are based on the lack of moral conformity to the teaching of the Church. This lack of conformity derives from the failure of true conversion.

iv. Christian Marriage and Christian Family. Until we have solid Christian marriages, we cannot count on true Christian families on which the local church is built. But the concept and practice of Christian marriage is precisely one of the greatest problems of the local churches. There is a general tendency to avoid Christian marriage according to the demands of canon law. According to one report,[6] at least half of the Christians of East Africa do not marry in church at all. According to this same report, one group of the East African countries, comprising Zambia and Zimbabwe, witness only one-third of their Christians marrying in church. In West Africa the situation is not at all better than in the East. In Ghana less than one quarter of the Catholics marry in church.

Everywhere in Africa there is no progress in the practice of Christian marriage. The Christian ideal of marriage is therefore situated in a social environment where traditional, cultural, moral, and economic factors militate against it from all sides. As a result we find that everywhere in our local communities the majority of the Christians are living in excommunication from full membership in the Church. Today the theme of marriage is the subject of special study and research in many dioceses. We have to join hands in these studies in order to find effective pastoral solutions for the future.

v. Effective Christian Witness in Public Life. The

interior spiritual life of the Church should not be hidden, but like a lamp should be raised high as a sign of salvation that is present and effective in the society. Indeed the credibility of the Church will depend a lot on her public image in the society. This demands of the members a sincere commitment to the moral principles of their faith and a personal witness to such principles in public life. West Africa is a network of young nations aspiring to political, economic, and social stability. Most of these young nations are facing serious political and economic crises: problems of injustice, corruption, and the violation of basic human rights.

In the face of these problems, Christians should show by their lives that there is no split between religion and public life. They are called upon to witness to the gospel message of justice, love, and peace. They must therefore engage themselves in action on behalf of justice and participate in the transformation of the world.[7] The dynamism of Christian witness will make visible the values that must shape men's lives and thereby bring about the required changes in the societies as well as in the individuals. Considering all this social background in which the Church has to live and function, she has the urgent task to make apostles of her members. In the actual situation, we have politicians who happen to be Christians but not Christian politicians, leaders who happen to be Christians but not Christian leaders; we have professionals who happen to be Christian but not Christian professionals.

The Church has the urgent task to reeducate and conscientise all her members in all walks of life to relate their faith to the social and political life. She should call on the intelligentsia to exercise their Christian responsibility in every sphere of life. The challenge of the present and of the future is one of interior and integral application of the gospel message. It is now a question of an effective Christian leadership that must permeate all spheres of life, including the socioeconomic sphere where social justice and interhuman relationships need redemption. This calls for the development of a Christian social doctrine that gives to the members of the Church a Christian vision of the world, economic activity, and society as a whole.

This type of witness calls for the active commitment of the local Church to speak for the poor and the oppressed and to renounce those privileges that identify her with the oppressors, the powerful, and the shamelessly rich. In fact many people in West Africa today look up to the Church to act as their spokesman in defence of their basic human rights and for the cause of justice. Now the organs for promoting these human rights and a Christian conscience in Africa are a Christian press, an enlightened lay apostolate, Christian youth organisations, and an effective adult education on the local and parochial level. In short it is a question of an effective Christian commitment and witness from the grass-root level where the enlightened members of the Church are rubbing shoulders with their fellow compatriots and are exerting a healthy influence on every aspect of life in the society.

4. THE CHALLENGE OF THE FUTURE: COLLABORATION, CONFORMITY, AND RESISTANCE

The urgent task of consolidating the Church can be seen as the greatest challenge of the African Church, especially at this turning point of the history of our young nations with their multiple problems on all levels. This challenge has to be taken very seriously, for from certain incidents in some countries, we can no longer rely on privilege. In fact one of the challenges of the future of the Church will be to give up all privileges, which were the result of fortuitous circumstances that are gone forever.

In the words of A. Hastings, this intuition is expressed in the following terms:

> To generalise, the vast work of evangelisation which has been accomplished in Africa during the last eighty years has been achieved within a situation and with means which we shall very soon have lost for good. The situation was one of privilege, sometimes gross over-privilege, of a near monopoly of the social services, and of an authority which in many places there should be seen no means of questioning. All this has gone. The Church no longer has privileges and monopolies, though she has often to suffer the backwash of having had them in the past; and the more she had, the more violent the reaction can be. Africans are coming to see today that the connection between the Church and schools was in some way fortuitous. . . . It does call for a reappraisal of our methods and priorities.[8]

It remains an urgent task of the mission of the Church to permeate all levels of society and transform them from within like leaven. The message of this mission is one of liberation, peace, justice, and universal brotherhood. This mission is to liberate men from the darkness of slavery, war, injustice, hatred, exploitation, and despair. By the very nature of this mission, the Church must be prepared for confrontation and even persecution if she is not to become conformist in a short-sighted way.

This catalystic role of the Church is very delicate and demands both prudence and courage in finding the right manner of permeating all the levels of society without unduly assuming the role of the State. This prudence, which demands at times confrontation, at times collaboration, and at times distance, is what Julius Nyerere meant when he said that the members of religious organisations must encourage and help the people to cooperate together in whatever action is necessary for the development of the people without regard to religion or denominational interest. Consequently where certain Church institutions involve her so much that this primary task is obscured, she must be ready to abandon them and concentrate on her primary mission. In this light let the Church not be unilaterally indentified with a given institution to the extent that it could not be conceived otherwise.

Furthermore this vision calls for the abolition of clerical paternalism that places the responsibility for most human affairs in the hands of the clergy alone. In fact it is impossible to have effective Christian leadership only in the hands of the clergy. Such leadership can be really effective only in the hands of committed lay people. It is the responsibility of committed lay people to promote social justice through their professional life and personal example. It is up to them to exercise the right leadership in bringing about the right type of trade unions and industrial relations in the interest of justice and equality.

It is only through the committed laity and their effective Christian leadership that we can realise in modern Africa the existence of an applied Christianity. Christianity without its social application is deformed and as such is useless for modern Africa. The challenge of the present and the future is the effectiveness of applied Christianity. It is therefore urgent for Christian leadership to permeate the socioeconomic sphere where social justice and interhuman relations need the redeeming power of the gospel. This urgent mission of the Church calls for a more elaborate formation of the laity so that they may be more imbued with the convictions of the gospel.

The question of confrontation and even persecution is not foreign to the Church of Christ. It has always been the strong conviction of the early Christians that the blood of martyrs is the seed of the Church from which springs forth the mysterious growth of the Church. Indeed the calibre of the local Church will be tested by her readiness to suffer hardships for the name of Christ and in defence of her convictions. Martyrdom is not possible without all those elements mentioned above. The many privileges that the Church in many places has inherited from the missionary and colonial era are indeed incompatible with the true nature and presence of the Church in any kind of society. Recent events in Ghana and other African countries show that the local Church must be prepared for confrontation and persecution.

The general trend in African politics since almost immediately after independence can be described as totalitarian and monolithic either in the leftist or rightist, socialist or capitalist directions. The one common characteristic in the recent developments is a strong ideological revolution with neocolonial elements. In this new development, it is evident that not only the privileges of the Church will be denied her but also her very existence will be challenged and this will sooner or later lead to persecution. It is therefore urgent for the local Church to prepare her members for persecution.

Lucas Abadanloora

NOTES

1. Walbert Buehlmann, *The Coming of the Third Church: An Analysis of the Present and Future of the Church,* English trans., (Slough: St. Paul Publications, 1976).

2. These figures are taken from the *Catholic Diary,* published by the
   Catholic Press of Accra. The second set of figures are taken from
   W. Buehlmann, *The Coming of the Third Church,* p. 129–130.
3. W. Buehlmann, *The Coming of the Third Church,* p. 152.
4. W. Buehlmann, *The Missions on Trial,* (Slough: St. Paul Publications, 1977), p. 130.
5. A. Hastings, *Church and Mission in Modern Africa* (London:
   1967), p.2.
6. A. Hastings, *Christian Marriage in Africa* (London: 1973).
7. From the Bishop's Synod, *Justice in the World,* (Rome: 1971).
8. A. Hastings, *Church and Mission in Modern Africa* (London:
   1967), p. 153.

Personalism: A Plea for the Person-Attitude in Life

There can be few vocations more interesting than that of seeking to understand the human person.
—*Paul Tournier*

In a very personal way, I came to be convinced of the truth that freedom is not so much the ability to choose between alternatives, but more an internal capacity to responsibly assume and direct the given conditions in which one finds oneself according to the set of values one has set for oneself.

Hence, though it was against my free choice that I applied myself to the study of philosophy—for I shared with most of you the conception (or is it a misconception) that philosophy is but an abstract speculation with no bearing on life—I could within the given situation, and through the medium of philosophy, bring myself to a deeper reflection on a problem that had always fascinated me—the meaning of human life.

My interest in this problem was aroused when in reading one of the books of John Poweel, I came across a curious design. This was the painting of a box, securely locked, and giving the impression of containing some heavy and precious good. On top of the box was the label "Human Beings, Handle with Care!" Sensitivity to the delicate character of the person is a prerogative to establishing any truly personal relation with him. This is only possible through a better knowledge of who man really is!

INTRODUCTION

Ordinarily, man, preoccupied by the daily cares for subsistence and the diversions of life, is hardly ever brought to question himself as to the meaning of his existence. It needs some extraordinary experience—some sickness, a great personal crisis, or some catastrophe—and man is immediately brought to a deep reflection on the meaning of his existence and of life in general. Martin Heidegger talks of the following three moods as metaphysical moments in man's life. They are first the mood of despair,

> (. . .) when things tend to lose all their weight and all meaning because obscured; (. . .), rejoicing, when all the things around us are transfigured and seem to be there for the first time, (. . .) and lastly boredom, when we are equally removed from despair and joy and everything about us seems so hopelessly commonplace that we no longer care whether anything is or is not . . .

At these times, man is forced to ask himself, Who am I? Why am I alive? Is there any meaning at all to human life, and to life in general?[1]

In the face of this metaphysical question revolving on my life as a human person, all other scientific questions shrink in importance. And yet paradoxically, if man can boast of some progress in his knowledge of the world in which he lives, the philosophical anthropologists attempting to come to some conclusive definition of man by collating all the information he has about man from the human sciences is eternally brought to despair. In fact, if Blaise

Pascal is right, man's quest for self-knowledge is a futile enterprise worth abandoning, for he says:

> Know then, proud man, what a paradox you are to yourself. Be humble, impotent reason! Be silent, feeble nature! Learn that man infinitely transcends man, hear from your Master your true condition which is unknown to you. Listen to God.[2]

According to this line of thought, reason should admit its impotence and only look to revelation to have some knowledge about our human condition. It is, however, our contention that if reason sees its task mainly as a reflection on the experiences of life in order to interpret and unify them to ascribe them with a meaning, such a task is not only imperative for man's self-knowledge, but also for his praxis.

The counsellor, the social worker, the psychiatrist, the priest, and all who engage in some service of the person, need a basis and finality for their engagements, a certain image of the person. Though the statement of Pascal brings out the fact that all attempts to characterise man must start with the awareness that man in his integrity is never fully present as an object of science, the certitude that there is some essence of man that should be respected in all our praxis is what is asserted by the personalist. The personalist claims that even if reason cannot have a full grasp of man, it can at least designate what is termed the "world of the person" by synthesising the partial truths he obtains from the glimpses he can have of man from his different stances of observation. It is then hoped that such knowledge, once obtained, should not only give us an idea of who we are, but should also guide us in our lives, i.e., we are brought to adopt the person-attitude in life, if we are to become more and more the person we are meant to be.

In this paper, we shall trace briefly the development of man's thinking of himself as presented in the history of philosophy. This shall lead us to focus on personalism as the philosophical school that best attempted to formulate the most integral ideas of man, and this, as represented by Emmanuel Mounier. Finally, we shall attempt to draw some practical conclusions on what the person-attitude as the main thrust of personalist thought, implies for us today.

I. REFLECTION ON MAN IN THE HISTORY OF PHILOSOPHY

Greek philosophy, which was born from a "wonder" at the mysteries of nature, could not but see man as being a part of nature. The cosmic laws of birth, life, death, decay, and new life, were seen to apply just as much to human life as to the other creatures. Hence, Theognis could assert with pessimism that it was best for man not to have been born and not to have seen the sight of the sun, but once born, the second best for him is to pass through the gates of death as speedily as may be.

Anaximander, for his part, claimed that according to the fundamental law of being, individual existence is an injustice, a guilt for which all men pay by returning to the source of their being in order to give room for others. For these philosophers, who saw certain death as the finality of human life, they could not ascribe it any meaning beyond this tragic end. Hence the absence of any real prescriptions for a moral life.

Real moral speculation on man's responsibility on earth will start with Socrates' *"gnothi seauthon"* (know yourself). In the *Symposium,* Socrates, in his allegorical language, tells us that man in the beginning was formed into a perfect circle and could revolve so fast that he could not be observed by the gods. Hence the gods split man into two to destroy his unobservable wholeness. Since then, according to Socrates, each man has been searching for his other half.

Eros (desire) is the expression of this will for unification in man. Its lowest expression is in sexual love, through which man looks for this unification and permanence. For Socrates, what man looks for especially in this eros is perfection, beauty, goodness, unity, which are always ultimately the things admired in the loved one. He contends that the soul's quest for beauty and these values, is a proof of its immortality. It is only the pre-existence of the soul in the world of ideas that can explain its reminiscence of these ideas that set it looking for the fulfilment of this drive in man.

Several conclusions can be drawn from this theory on the moral thought of Socrates. First, man as a mortal and inferior being to the gods, must always beware of the jealousy of the gods—know yourself, that you are only a mortal and not a god. This knowledge should keep you from any false pride, which could be punished by the gods. Second, man is a being that transcends himself and does not see his end in this earthly existence. Through eros, he can transcend his individual existence not only by continuing to exist in his descsendants, but also in his spiritual activity (knowledge). Third, the human soul is immortal and hence does not perish with his body.

However, with Aristotle, the philosopher who has influenced most our Christian thought through Saint Thomas, it is the naturalistic conception of man that comes again to the fore.

Seeing man against the background of the cosmos,

Aristotle believed that the whole of the cosmos is engaged in a motion towards a final goal. In this connection, he talks of two modes of motion—transitive motion, that is caused by an external agent, and immanent motion, caused by the internal dynamism of the living creature. Whilst the ultimate cause of external motion is said to be Unmoved Mover, Aristotle appeals to the principle of the soul to explain the internal motion. Hence his talk of the vegetative and sensitive souls in plants and animals, respectively. Man who has vegetative, sensitive, and rational qualities, is said to have a triple soul. But Aristotle is fast to add that in as far as man is a single substance, there is no division between these aspects of his life. In fact the vegetative and sensitive aspects of man are subsumed to his rational life, which is the very form or essence of man as man!

This notion of the one soul as giving form to the body of man is much in conformity with Aristotle's principle of individuation, in which he insists that the individual is that which makes a thing having the same nature as another differ from this other thing of the same species and genus, and differ from another thing of which it shares the same nature. Thus, he could apply this notion of individuality—that which is in itself indistinct but distinct from all other things—not only to man, but to whatever being there is, be it a plant, an animal, or a human being.

If Aristotle thus speaks of soul like Plato, the soul for him is not seen so much as a separate transcendent reality. It is much more a philosophical principle needed to explain the observable activities in man. In fact, in as far as the soul is the form of the body, it is consonant with Aristotelian thought to assert that the soul is incapable of existing without the body and must necessarily perish with it. (This is not to disregard the debate among

Aristotle scholars about the idea of immortality in Aristotle's philosophy from his notion of the *nous* as the light of reason.)

It is with the Stoics that we find for the first time the use of the term "person" in philosophical anthropology. For the Stoics, the Greek term *"prosopon,"* used to designate the mask as a device to fake personalities in drama, was seen as being very apt to illustrate the situation of man in the universe. The world for the Stoics is a grand stage on which we are all character or "personna" in the scene of life. As visitors, we are all expected to act our life-scenes with indifference. True happiness therefore lies in expecting that the worst can always happen to you. In that case, nothing, no matter how tragic or painful, can be seen as a source of sadness. Since we are all insincere actors, it is no crime to treat the other we meet on earth as mere objects of "play." Such a view of the person is a very far cry from what it will come to stand for in Judeo-Christian tradition.

With the Roman jurists, the term "personna" comes to stand for the moral person as the subject of moral rights and obligations. It will then be taken over by Boethius and the Christian theologians of the Middle Ages to explain the trinitarian relations.[3] In this context, the person is then seen as the source and beneficiary of the free activity of love.

Thomas Aquinas, taking up the definition given by Boethius, speaks of the person as an "individual substance rational by nature."[4] He will, however, go on to insist that since through his spiritual faculties, man alone is capable of freedom and love, he alone, as the most perfect creature and image of God, can be termed person—in the manner of the persons of the Trinity.

From the foregoing historical sketch, the following

conclusions can be tentatively drawn: First, that philosophers have tended to see man from a purely naturalistic point of view as being a part of nature—most exemplified by the Greek philosophers and Aristotle.

Second, though Plato and Aristotle speak of the soul, we should desist from immediately identifying this principle with the soul we are used to speaking about in Christian tradition. While Plato saw the immortal soul as the best means to explain his theory of knowledge and man's transcendence, Aristotle saw it more as a principle necessary to explain observable activities in living things, without ascribing a separate existence to it. That the soul cannot outlive the dissolution of the body argues against any attempt to prove the immortality of the soul from Aristotle's philosophy.

Though the term "person" was used from the Stoic period on, one has the impression that it was more current in theological discussions than in philosophy. Philosophers tended to see man more as an individual, a substance, definable from an ontological point of view, rather than as a person, with its connotations of love and freedom. Was it because of the theological connotations of the term? Even in political and social philosophy, where freedom of the individual and his rights became a topic for discussion, freedom was envisioned more as a natural right of the individual possessed as a good, which he could dispose of by way of a contract (see especially the Contract philosophers like Rousseau and Hobbes).

Justice within this model of man as a monadic individual, is defined from an egalitarian perspective. Each individual is seen as an atom in the whole body of the social entity (an artificial creation), and each man lays claim to the equal rights of self-preservation. Without any regard to personal differences and inequality of opportunity, it is believed that justice is created by equality (egalitarianism). It is this atomistic individualism with its inherent optimism and egalitarianism that is at the base of both liberal democracy and Marxism. It will be the aim of the personalists to replace the individual at the base of the social and political thought of the time with the person as a more integral designation of the full reality of man.

It was the face of the crisis of the Western Civilization in the 1930s that Jacques Maritain, in a bid to apply his Christian principles in seeking for solutions to the social problems, brought out the distinction between "individual" and "person" in philosophy. Jacques Maritain held that "the distinction between the individual and the person applied in the relations between man and the state contained in the domain of the metaphysical principles, the solution to most of the social problems."[5] Using the term individual and person as ontological categories, he stated that whilst the individual forms part of society, society as such is ordered to the service of the person whose finality is in God.

The leitmotif of the 1930s thus became, "the individual for society and the society for the person."[6] This was to express the conviction that if the state as a whole is superior to the individual, it must desist from imposing itself as an absolute over the person since its main task is to provide the human being—the person—with the best possible conditions to realise his personal and spiritual life. It was thus the hope of these Catholic thinkers to be able to fight both individualism and communism in political life by investigating into the total world of the person. Personalism, as the school of thought aimed at designating the total universe of the person, could then provide men with an integral humanism as the basis and finality of their engagements.

II. THE PERSONALIST VISION OF MAN: INTEGRAL HUMANISM

Though the term "person" as a metaphysical category was introduced into social and political thought by Jacques Maritain, it is with Emmanuel Mounier (1905–1950) that personalism as a philosophical school in France will emerge. If Mounier believed that the crises of the 1930s were the result of the false humanism underlying the political and economic systems of his day, he was convinced that only the system of thought that presented politicians with an integral humanism, for their engagements could rescue man from the contemporary oppressions he was experiencing under liberal democracy, communism, and fascism.

Mounier's personalism was therefore an attempt to draw from all relevant sources, whatever truth he could find about man, in order to synthesise these truths into a total vision on man.

As a convinced Catholic who saw his philosophical enterprise as a vocation to "combat for the (total) person,"[7] he will be first and foremost inspired in all his works by the Gospels and the Christian social teaching. In this regard he will draw very much from Thomistic theology on the notion of the person and related topics. A second source of influence will be that of the Existentialist philosopher Gabriel Marcel. Against idealism, the Existentialists had begun to stress the need for philosophy to centre on the concrete human person in its reflections. Philosophy should descend from its abstract speculation on "a priori," eternal essences to the reality that is historical and dynamic.

As regards the person, two thoughts of the Existentialists were to play an important role in Mounier's thought—namely that as a being in history, man can never be an object of knowledge. For something to be fully grasped in knowledge, it has to be fully presented to the subject of observation. This means that as long as both subject and object are caught in the process of history, it would be futile to attempt to have a full grasp of the person.

Related to this first intuition of the Existentialists is their belief that if man can never be objectified, we cannot then speak of an "essence" in man as some static quality that reason could point to. If there is anything like an essence, in the human person, it is his freedom as a subject, which is referring more to his manner of existence than to an objectifiable quality. A third source of influence will be the moral philosophy of Max Scheller. Not only his phenomenological method (the method of description from partial glimpses, and not characterisation), but especially his vision of man as a being of relations (the community aspect in man) will be taken over my Mounier.

Drawing on all the above sources, Mounier's reflection on the person will always have as its background the political situation of the 1930s—a situation that he will hope to negate through his personalism. The political evils brought to light by the crises will serve as the negative influences that spur Mounier on to designate his world of the person—the integral humanism we now proceed to describe.

The real/concrete man is a world of relations that integrates his material, personal, communitarian, and transcendent dimensions into a unified whole. If the liberalist and the communist each presents some truth about man, their fallacy lies in the undue stress they give to one or the other aspect of man to the neglect of the others. Integral humanism must hold together the following truths about man:

a) Man as Incarnate Existence

Against any denigration of the body, as found in some spiritualisms, the personalist affirms that man is wholly body and wholly spirit. Through his body, he not only forms a part of nature, but is present wherever his body is. It is true that the body can be a source of alienation like anything else, but this is not to say that the body by virtue of its material character is the tomb of the spirit. Furthermore, my body is not just an object I possess. It is through my body that I think; I expose myself through my body (the face). The material world annexes itself to my body, and in thus sharing my destiny, necessarily transcends its mere materiality in my spiritual acts, which would not be possible without my body.

Hence the conviction of the personalists that in as far as the material world is caught up in man's move to personalization, it has a transcendent character. This means that man, though material in his bodily existence, is not merely material. He is called upon to live the tension of dispersion into matter, and transcendence in his spiritual activities exposed through his body. Herein lies the basic fallacy of any materialistic conception of man that would tend to disregard this dialectic in the person.

b) The Communitarian Dimension of Man

If my body is in a sense very much linked to my personal identity, it is true to say that my existence as a person necessarily implies the existence of the other. It is only in the face of the other as not being myself that I can affirmatively say 'I.'

I do not only need the other to be able to affirm myself existentially, but even my development as a person is impossible without the other. How much we are daily formed not only by our parents and peers, but also by what Sartre refers to as the "look of the other." (Consciously or unconsciously, the feeling of being approved or disapproved by the anonymous observer plays a lot on what we do or refuse to do.) All this goes to say that to be a person implies an openness to the other. The I-thou relation established in a dialogue between persons is an indication of the community dimension in man. Max Scheller goes as far as to say that man's ability to relate with others in community stems from the "common factor" present in each person enabling him to form a community of persons with others.

If however we say man is a community being, we should desist from identifying this quality with all forms of collectivism that deny the uniqueness of each man, thus subsuming the personal identity into some collective spirit or mind. True community should make for the growth of each member in his personhood without which we cannot speak of true dialogue among the members of the community. It should work towards forming a community describable as a "person of persons."[8]

c) Man as a Unique Individual

As pointed out above, the person needs to maintain his identity if he is to enter into any meaningful dialogue with members of his community. It is this internal quality of the person to be able to withdraw into himself in order to exteriorize what is most personal of himself to the other in a dialogue that most indicated the levels of one's maturity. Through an internal meditation alone is one capable of setting for oneself values, necessary for a creative authentic living. It is also in this internal or intimate conversion on oneself that one is able to solve the dialectic tensions of daily existence. Hence the personalists believe that freedom is not so much the absence of external coercion, but more an internal quality—namely, the manner in which one assumes and gives personal meaning to the conditions that make up his history.

d) Man as a Transcending Being

From the above, we realise that from whatever perspective of description, man is always seen to be the observable and more. Though each of the relations described above is essential in the description of man, the person always transcends each particular one of them. Hence Malebranche can talk of man as that being engaged in a "constant movement to always go further."[9]

For Mounier, this perpetual move to transcendence cannot be without purpose. In this regard, the difference between the atheistic Existentialist and the theist is not that one believes in transcendence and the other does not. It is rather in the fact that whilst the atheist claims that it is a transcendence to nothingness, the theist sees the finality of this move in a personal being. In as far as both positions are ultimately dependent on one's philosophical faith, I would see more logic in believing that a world caught in a move towards personalization finds its fulfilment in some personal being. Without this conviction, which gives some objective backing to the belief in the spiritual character of man, it becomes difficult to justify any dignity in man worth fighting for. The denial of the Transcendent necessarily brings in its trend the denial of the transcendence in man; is it therefore surprising that atheistic humanists end up oppressing the very person they started out to combat for?

III. THE PERSON-ATTITUDE IN LIFE

What emerges from the above is that according to the personalists, the person is seen as a web of relations comprising of the material, the social, the transcendent, and the individual "personages."[10]

Not only is a full concord between the person and any of these personages an impoverishment of the person, more than that, it fails to realize that the person as a historical being is constantly caught up in the tensions and dialogues of these opposing personnages. That is why to live a truly personal life demands a daily strive to resolve the internal crises by reference to the hierarchy of values one has set for oneself. Paul Tounier puts it succinctly when he says,

> In this world, full concord between personnages and person remains an utopian ideal. Further, by an odd paradox we approach it only in so far as we become day by day more aware of their constant discord. So that we might also say that progress in our knowledge of ourselves is progess from uneasiness to uneasiness. (. . .) The final reality of the person, always in motion—complex, mysterious and incomprehensible—still eludes us. This tension that always exists between the person and the personage is one of the conditions of our life, and we must accept it. It is part of the nature of man—indeed, what makes him a man.[11]

To realize that the person is never fully characterizable (hence the pretentious character of the empirical psychologist's attempt to categorise men in types) is an important intuition on man. To see the person as basically caught in a tension of relations that make up his world, and to assert a hierarchy of values that would safeguard the transcendence of man in his dialogue with others and nature, is basically what is meant by the person-attitude of the personalist philosophers.

According to Paul Ricoeur, the person-attitude is "the realization that the person is this entity for whom the notion of crisis is the essential repertoire of his situation."[12] This realization forces me to constantly reassert a stable hierarchy of values in a sometimes confused world, for the creation of a more and more person-orientated world. This is not without its practical consequences, as we shall go on to show.

PRACTICAL CONCLUSIONS

For the sake of brevity, we would like to elucidate rather briefly on what this person-attitude would imply for us in three spheres of our lives. These are, namely, the personal, socio-political, and technological aspects of our relations.

To adopt the person-attitude in life is to live in humility. Since truth is always dialectical, no one person from his partial stance can claim knowledge of the whole truth. There is, therefore, the need for openness to dialogue and for a constant self-criticism. In the second place, it warns us against fixing a "character" on someone, thus failing to admit the dynamic and mysterious dimensions in his life. The Christian exhortation "Thou shall not judge" gets its philosophical backing in this trend of thought.

In the sphere of politics, personalism's plea for a person-attitude is in contradiction to the rule by an ideology. Jean Lacroix, in his book *Le personnalisme comme anti-idéologie,* shares the opinion of Gabriel Marcel that

> an ideology by its nature aspires to become a propaganda and only takes flesh on condition that it exercises itself against a certain category of people. . . . in the pejorative

sense, an ideology becomes a more or less coherent system of ideas which a group presents as an exigence of reason, but of which the effective motive lies in the need to satisfy and to justify their particular interests.[13]

Our world is divided between East and West, communism versus liberalism, nearer home, our African continent is raged with revolutions and coups d'etat, made in the name of the people or the suffering masses. What one discovers is that at the base of all these political activities is some ideology and not the person. The tragedy lies in the fact that these ideologies, though they always present some truth about the human person, tend to absolutise their position, thus shutting out any possibility for dialogue with other viewpoints.

Speaking about the need to revert to the person as the base and finality of all political action, Etienne Borne[14] asserts that democracy and communism must always go together as the conditions of possibility for posing political questions in an honest manner, since they bring out the individual and communitarian aspects of man. According to him, whilst democracy in its formalism calls for the maintenance of the tension between freedom and justice by laying stress on the unique character of the individual, communism lays its fundamental stress on the important tension of the individual and society. Hence just as the individual and society go in pairs, there can be no true socialism or communism without democracy and vice versa. Only a continual dialogue between communism/socialism and democracy would be the source of dynamism and continual reform of our political structures for the sake of the person.

Herein lies the role of the Church in politics. True though it is that the Church is not expected to take up the reins of government, it is the duty of the Church to constantly point to the ideal of the integral person as the finality of all political action. Against the tendency of governments to settle on some ideology that they defend in place of the person, the Church serves as a constant reminder that the dynamism and ultimate justification for political authority lies in the defence of the integral person.

In the field of science and technology, we can say that today the objectivating spirit of the empirical sciences is fast invading the sphere of the so-called human sciences. There tends to be the feeling that only that intellectual enterprise that is empirically verifiable or justifiable can lay claim to being a science. Hence the emptying of the person of all his spiritual qualities, or at best, the relegation of the spiritual to the religious, in order to treat man as an object of science.

Concretely this is seen in the normalcy with which the idea of the test-tube baby is taken, the use of human species for laboratory experiments in medicine are all cases in point. In the field of technology, the robot is fast competing with man for employment. The person-attitude in science calls for a reappraisal of man's position in the universe. If there are reasons for us to believe that man as a transcendent being is the apex of nature in its move for personalization, no individual person can be treated as an object. If our world tends to lose its meaning or significance, it may be because man as the creature that gives meaning or sense to nature is fast losing his senses.

The strongest objection to man as a transcendent or spiritual being giving sense to nature normally comes from the empirical circles. These empiricists claim that there is no observable quality or experience in man that would justify such a vision about man. The fallacy of such a view is that it limits observable experience to "experimental experience." But phenomenologists have felt the need to broaden the notion of experience in our description of such human experiences as love, anxiety, and trust into our philosophical reflections about man. If these experiences point to the "more than observable" elements in the human person, the acceptance or denial of the spiritual or transcendent in man stems more from one's philosophical faith rather than from any conclusive arguments for or against it.

It is for this reason that we believe that at least from the philosophical point of view, the person remains the best candidate for intercultural as well as interpersonal dialogue. I must, however, admit that the greatest sin of personalism and its person-attitude is its seeming forgetfulness of the role of sin in man. It calls for a continual optimism, even in the face of a crisis-laden world. Maybe this attitude is necessary since, as Mounier rightly pointed out, to be discouraged about man is to discourage him! From our Christian faith, we would even go further to see this optimism as *the* attitude to life. After all, are we not constantly challenged to point beyond the darkness to the gleam of light, beyond the cross to the Resurrection!

Edward B. Tengan

NOTES

1. Martin Heidegger, *An Introduction to Metaphysics*, trans. Ralph Manheim (London: Yale University Press, 1980), p. 1.
2. Blaise Pascal, *Pensées*, trans. A.J. Krailsheimer, (Middlesex: Penguin Books Ltd, 1977), p. 64–65.
3. The use of the term "person" to translate the Greek *hypostasis* was to cause a great rift between the Greek and Latin Churches. This misunderstanding stemmed from the difference in philosophical tradition underlying the interpretation of the relation Substance-person!
4. Thomas Aquinas; *Summa Theologiae*, Ia, q. 29, a. 3.
5. Jacques Maritain, "Le Roseau d'Or," *Trois Réformateurs: Luther,*

Descartes, Rousseau, (Paris: Librairie Plon, 1925), p. 32.

6. Roger Benjamin, *Notions de personne et personnalisme Chrétien,* (Paris: Mouton, 1971), p. 114.

7. Emmanuel Mounier, *Oeuvres,* 4 vols. (Paris: Editions du Seuil, 1961–1963), Vol. II, *Traité du caractère,* Introduction.

8. According to Mounier, a truly personalist community that is based on all the human values necessary for the total growth of the human person can be called a "person of persons" (cf. *Oeuvres,* Vol. 1, p. 202).

9. Nicolas Malebranche, *Oeuvres,* "Bibliothèque de la Pléiade," Vol. 1 (Paris:Gallimard, 1979), p. 29 et alia, a leitmotif of the author.

10. Paul Tournier, *The Meaning of Persons* (London: SCM Press, 1978). In Part One of this book, the author speaks at length about the personage and how it is distinct from the person. We adopt this term to bring out the distinction between the partial glimpse on man (personage) and the person as such. We feel it a better distinction than the person-individual distinction.

11. Ibid., p. 83.

12. Paul Ricoeur, "Meurt le personnalisme, revient la personne," in *"Cinquantenaire" Esprit* (January 1983, Paris), p. 116–117.

13. Jean Lacroix, *Le personnalisme comme anti-idéologie,* "Collection SUP" no. 105, (Paris: Presse Universitaires de France, 1972), p. 12.

14. Etienne Borne, "Les options du personnalisme depuis 50 ans, vis-à-vis de la démocratie," *Colloque Cinquantenaire,* Le personalisme d'Emmanuel Mounier hier et demain. (transcribed from my personal recordings).

Some Theological Reflections of Africans after the Independence of Black Africa

Preamble

After twenty-seven years of independence, it is imperative that we here in Ghana ask ourselves questions that deal with our basic needs, such as food, shelter, health, education, culture, and even religion. What have we achieved politically? What have we achieved economically? What have we achieved socially, and what are our religious and moral achievements? Unless we make an objective analysis of our independence, our political, economic, social, cultural, and religious principles cannot, as they should, have any reference to the needs and nature of our liberated territories. Second, in assessing the independence of Ghana, we cannot do that in isolation since Ghana's independence set the pace for the rest of Africa, which was under colonial rule.

After all, quite a number of us can still recall the Pan-African slogan of Kwame Nkrumah, which says: "The independence of Ghana is meaningless unless it is linked up with the total liberation of Africa." It is with these two principles in view that I would like to assess the religious or theological thinking of Africans after the attainment of independence. This theological reflection will touch on how the Africans are trying to make religion and theology relevant for the African. It will touch on the efforts of theologians to deal with the knotty and obnoxious problems of Apartheid in South Africa.

Thus I shall be touching on the theological reflection of Africans on their culture, which is given the name of African Inculturation Theology; I shall be dealing with the need of liberation, which we still stand in need of even after the attainment of political independence; and finally I shall touch on a very pertinent form of liberation that we in Ghana still need.

INTRODUCTION

A theme often on the lips of African bishops and theologians since the independence of their countries is Africanisation. The independent fervour of the late 1950s and the early 1960s contributed to a new awareness and felt need for the realisation of the newly acquired independence in all its aspects. Certain heads of states have even spoken of the need to reaffirm the identity and authenticity of African culture. By that they mean that the African must assert himself as such and not merely be a black European.

In the eyes and words of many such politicians, the Church to whom they owe their education is seen as an imported product that Africa must learn to do without. People were told to replace the European suit and tie in a hot climate with a more culturally designed dress that was better suited to our climate. Architects were told to get inspiration from traditional building patterns. African musicians and dramatists were encouraged by vigorous promotion of their art and the consequent new taste for African music and cultural dance.

Even Church men were not spared from the political

86

wind of change. They were told to stop giving foreign saint names to those they were baptizing; and those who were already baptized either freely dropped their foreign saint names in favour of indigenous names or they were forced into it by the enthusiastic politicians. The African bishops themselves sought to adopt this wind of change blowing across Black Africa.

They invited the Christians to purify the Church of what is Western and conserve only what is Catholic. They asked the faithful to love their religion in the context of the culture of the African continent. There were a number of theologians, particularly in Zaire, who advocated for the replacement of the Mass wine by palm wine or *pito* and the eucharistic bread by some suitable African cake, such as our *Maasa*. It was in these circumstances that African theology was born.

To speak of African theology is to touch the complex problem of ethnology and religion in the African continent. It means defining the terms "African" and "Theology." When the term "African" is coterminous with the continent that bears this name, then the concept "African" must include the Arabs living in North Africa, the peoples of the Negroid race living in Africa south of the Sahara, and the peoples of European and Asian origin living mostly in South Africa. This rich complexity of ethnic groupings brings with it the multiplicity of religions, cultures, and languages.

Three main types of religion may be discerned in Africa: Christianity, Traditional African Religion, and Islam. Just as there are various denominations and sects within Christianity and Islam, so also are there various forms of Traditional African Religion. Thus to evolve a *Theologia Africana* meeting linguistic, social, cultural, political, economic, and the deep religious needs of the *homo Africanus* is to undertake the Herculean task of killing a "multiheaded hydra."[1] African Christian Theologians have, however, begun to undertake this seemingly impossible task.

AFRICAN THEOLOGY: A HISTORICAL SKETCH

The question that comes to the mind of any theologian is: Can African theologians evolve a theology that will see to give answers to the social, political, cultural, economic, and deep-seated religious aspiration of this vast continent and yet remain faithful to the Gospel and its rich Christian heritage? What have Africans to learn from their forefathers of the early Christian Church? Can the African Christian theologian build up a theology that at once avoids the errors of Origen and Tertullian and yet incorporates the genius of Cyril of Alexandria and the outstanding African Church Father, Saint Augustine of Hippo? To evolve such an African Theology is to plunge into a formidable task.

Since the launching of African Theology, three major theological currents have so far emerged: African Inculturation Theology, Black Theology, and Liberation Theology. For a long time, African Inculturation Theology was coterminous with African Theology. Most African theologians were mostly concerned with conducting a fruitful and meaningful dialogue with African Traditional Religions.

Both the sceptists[2] and the enthusiasts[3] of African theology drew a lot of comfort from the speech of Pope Paul VI delivered in Rubaga Cathedral, Kampala, on the first day of his historic visit to Africa in 1969. Among other things the Pope said:

> The expression, that is, the language and mode of manifesting this one Faith may be manifold, hence it may be original, suited to the tongue, the style, the character, the genius and the culture of the ones who profess this one Faith. From this point of view, a certain pluralism is not only legitimate, but desirable. An adaptation of the Christian life in the fields of pastoral, ritual, didactic and spiritual activities is not only possible, it is even favoured by the Church. The liturgical renewal is a living example of this. And in this sense you may, and you must, have an African Christianity. Indeed you possess human values and characteristic forms of culture which can rise up to perfection so as to find in Christianity, and for Christianity, a true superior fullness and prove to be capable of a richness of expression all its own, and genuinely African.[4]

In conclusion, the Pope urged Africans to bring "to the Catholic Church the precious and original contribution of 'negritude,' which she needs particularly in this historic hour."[5]

Although the Pope's appeal was mostly directed to Roman Catholics, his use of "African Christianity" and the philosophical term "negritude" rekindled the discussion on African Theology. In the same year that the Pope visited Uganda, the Protestant organisation of the All-Africa Conference of Churches, meeting in Abidjan, Ivory Coast, declared:

> African Theology is a theology based on the Biblical faith of Africans, and which speaks to the African soul. It is expressed in categories of thought which rise out of the philosophy of the African people. This does not mean it is narrow in outlook (syncretistic). To speak of African

Theology involves formulating clearly a Christian attitude to other religions. . . . [6]

One can almost sense a Pan-African theology in this declaration.

Writing ten years after the declaration of the All-Africa Conference of Churches, John S. Pobee, a professor of New Testament and Church History at the University of Ghana, takes a rather sober look at African Theology and defines it as follows: "African Theology is concerned to interpret essential Christian Faith in authentic African language in the flux and turmoil of our time so that there may be genuine dialogue between Christian faith and African cultures."[7]

Pobee is thus joining the chorus of African theologians who are not so much calling for adaptation of Christianity to African culture and mentality, but above all for indigenisation, inculturation, and incarnation of Christianity. But it is not clear whether Pobee's application of his definition of African Theology to the Akan people of Ghana—one of at least fourteen major ethnic groups of this small country—is meant as a "paradigmatic of a type"[8] or as a "thorough and academically effective and profitable" study as has been advocated by Professor Idowu.[9] In any event, no one more than Pobee has realised the by-nigh impossibility of evolving a single meaningful theology for so vast a continent embracing at least 745 distinct languages and variations of cults and traditions in bewildering numbers. Must we then give up the quest for an African Theology?

HISTORICAL LINKS WITH THE BIBLE?

Let it be remembered that the complex structures of the various ethnic groups do not in reality pose such an insurmountable problem, for the differences have been and continue to be eroded by interaction. Recent quantitative analysis of rock-art samples from study areas in the northern and southern regions of Africa have shown surprising similarities. Besides the linguistic evidence, the study of oral, historical traditions, the analysis of myths, folk-tales, proverbs, incantations, praise-names, and songs have all revealed a high degree of interaction between different ethnic groups. Moreover, the achievements of African and European historians have provided evidence for the diffusion of religious ideas and for cross-cultural contacts on, at least, a limited basis.[10]

In this connection, it might be noted how studies carried out by Evans-Pritchard on Nuer religion,[11] Lienhardt on the religion of the Dinka,[12] and the French White Father Père Girault on the religion of the Dagara[13] have revealed startling similarities of beliefs and religious concepts. The results are, however, not too startling for the present writer, who belongs to the tribe of the Dagara.

For the Dagara, who inhabit the area stretching from the southwest of Burkina Faso to the northwest of Ghana, recall in their oral tradition and myths that a people called the Djani once dwelt in their land.[14] Other studies have shown that the Djani are to be associated with the ancient Niger basin town of Dya, which is located in the Mandingo area. Since the Nuer and the Dinka are also found in this region, it is no wonder that Evans-Pritchard and Lienhardt should arrive at findings closer to those arrived at by Girault in his study of the Dagara.

A further research conducted by Dieterlen on the area stretching from the Niger basin to the West Coast of Africa has demonstrated the existence of commercial and pilgrim routes between the Mandingo area and the present-day Ghana.[15] He has shown that the Dogon, or the Djani, had to leave the south of Sudan in about the thirteenth century A.D. because they did not want to convert to Islam.[16] From his earlier works and from the geographical research of Mauny, [17] Dieterlen has noted the indisputable links between the Niger basin and the Mediterranean Sea in ancient times.

But the question that spontaneously springs up is: how far back do these links go? The maps and works consulted by R. Mauny seem to go back to pre-literary times and do show numerous communication routes crisscrossing the Sahara. That would lead us to conclude that the communication links between North Africa and the Niger Basin on the one hand, and those between the Niger Basin and the West Coast of Africa on the other hand, were fairly frequent and date back to very ancient times. This assumption is further corroborated by the fact that the name of the Supreme Being for many African tribes is etymologically bound up with the sun,[18] and thus reminding us of the ancient Egyptian god Re.

If the foregoing assumptions are correct, then a number of interesting questions arise. Did the Christian Bible as such never cross the Sahara in ancient times? Did Christianity, which flourished in North Africa and produced such giants as Origen, Tertullian, Cyril of Alexandria, Augustine of Hippo, etc., remain the sole property of North Africans or did it even in these early years also cross over to Black Africa? Are the so-called "seeds of revelation," which are present in many traditional African religions, the result of the innate religiosity of man or are they not rather the vestiges of Judeo-Christian revelation that has undergone changes because of social, cultural, linguistic, and other environmental conditions?

Could some of the African traditional religions not

be typical examples of thoroughgoing and unhampered indigenisation, inculturation, or incarnation of Judeo-Christian religion? In point of fact, some of the independent African churches, which are off-shoots of the traditional Christian churches, seem to provide answers for the above questions. Church historians have thus got a lot of research and thinking to do on this too-long-neglected aspect of African Church history. Such a study will not only serve to explain the presence of common religious elements in most African traditional religions, it will also help to evolve a theology that is genuinely African and yet universal.

In the meantime, however, Christianity must continue to conduct a meaningful dialogue with African traditional religions. This is all the more necessary in such burning issues as the Supreme Being, the sacredness of life, the sense of community, and the world of the spirits. A hasty identification of the African Supreme Being with Yahweh, God of Israel, or with the Father of Our Lord, Jesus Christ, have often resulted in Christians and African traditional religionists talking at different wavelengths. Since African Christians are not spared from this misunderstanding, a meaningful dialogue will benefit both the African Christian and the traditional religionist.

BLACK THEOLOGY

While the attainment of independence by the majority of African states has given rise to African Theology of Inculturation, the non-attainment of independence is the background for Black Theology in South Africa.

The apartheid policy of South Africa has prepared a very fertile ground for Black Theology. The name has been adopted wholesale, but the methods, strategies, and principles are a little different from Black Theology as it is known in the U.S.A. Allan Aubrey Boesak, one of the prominent South African black theologians, gives his version of Black Theology as follow:

> Black Theology is the understanding of the Gospel of Jesus Christ within a black situation. Black Theology is a Theology of Liberation. . . . One can say that it presents a new way of theologising, a new manner of believing. Since Liberation Theology begins with the Exodus and brings theology to a critical reflection on the liberation praxis, it presents the Gospel in its authentic perspective, namely, liberation: as the Gospel of the poor.[19]

As the burden of segregation and oppression weighs heavily on the indigenous Black Africans and they feel humiliated and dejected, a natural reaction of rejecting the oppressor and all that goes with him is understandable.

The oppressive regime of South Africa is wrongly but understandably indentified with the white race. In his latest book, *Unschuld, die Schuldig Macht,*[20] Boesak describes what it means to be black in South Africa:

> Blackness is a reality which involves the totality of the black man's existence. . . . Blackness condemns him to live as a second class citizen. . . . Blackness determines his whole life, every single day. It entails living in constant fear, liable to inhuman treatment and humiliation; one has to live from the "grace" of those who for three hundred years have shown that they have no idea whatever of what that word means. The black man in South Africa is classified as a non-white: a non-person, less than the white man and thus a lesser human being.

Black Theology thus becomes the attempt to depict and reinterpret Christianity in terms of a liberating force in the context of segregation and oppression.

Even though Boesak is at one with his counterparts in the U.S.A. in his emphatic affirmation of the equality of blacks and whites before God and the blacks' refusal to be designated as non-whites, he has, nevertheless parted company with American Black Theologians with respect to the apartheid problem in South Africa.

He sees the solution of the problem of apartheid as the primary duty of all Christian churches in South Africa irrespective of race, colour, or confession. In a much-publicised address to the 1979 National Conference of South African Churches, Allan Boesak said:

> The Church must initiate and support meaningful pressure on the system as non-violent way of bringing about change. The Church must initiate and support programmes of civil disobedience on a massive scale, and challenge especially white Christians on this issue. It no longer suffices to make statements condemning unjust laws as if nothing has happened. The time has come for the black Church to tell the Government and its people: We cannot in all good conscience obey your unjust laws because non-cooperation with evil is much a moral obligation as is cooperation with good. So we will teach our people what it means to obey God rather than man in South Africa.[21]

AFRICAN LIBERATION THEOLOGY

A late-comer to the forum of African Theology is Liberation Theology, which makes its way to Africa through Latin American theologians who spearheaded the Association of Third World Theologians. Liberation Theology is becoming increasingly popular, especially in these days when more and more states are being ruled by radical army officers of the junior rank.

True to its ancestor, African Liberation Theology has as many undercurrents as there are in Latin America. One is therefore not surprised that certain brands of African Liberation Theology uncritically adopt Marxist-Leninist terminologies to formulate their theologies. For these theologians, scientific socialism represents the most fruitful and far-reaching approach to the integral liberation of man. They would even go to the extent of accepting class warfare as an indispensable tool of Liberation Theology. Sometimes the political and economic situation of a country becomes so pathological that one can at least sympathize with those, who having lost all hope in the transforming influence of Christianity, humanitarian reformism, and political action, turn to violence as the last and desperate resource.

It is, however, common knowledge that the so-called revolutionaries who start off with the grandiose intent of establishing the dictatorship of the proletariat sooner or later end up by being more atrocious and horrifying than the dictators and exploiters they have replaced. A violent revolution, even if it takes on the name Christian, introduces into society a chain of endless revolutions until the sons and daughters of the revolutionaries themselves are devoured and wiped out from the face of the earth. No revolution is worth the name unless of heart and mentality. Hence the indispensable prerequisite for restructuring the country and the world in which we live is a radical, all-embracing Christian METANOIA.

AUTHENTIC LIBERATION OF THE AFRICAN

Without downplaying the importance of sound theological thinking for a radical, social, economic, and political liberation of the *homo Africanus* and without underestimating the impact that such a sound theology should have on the regrettably servile and inhuman treatment to which several Africans and especially women are still being subjected, there is the need to stress the liberating role of theology for the *homo Africanus* whose daily life is still unduly dominated by an excessive fear of the evil spirits and witchcraft. The leader of the elemental spirits who is still highly enthroned in the African spirit world has got to be dethroned.

The fear of evil spirits and witches is so ingrained in Africa south of the Sahara that even enlightened men and women are not spared from it. A sick person will first consult the sorcerer before he goes to the doctor. It is not seldom to find even a medical doctor attributing some form of sicknesses to the evil eye of the witch. Politicians who profess to be Christians or even atheists are sometimes found wearing amulets or keeping supposedly powerful deities to protect them against evil spirits and the machinations of the witches. In Ghana, at least, the *Kramo* has become a dreaded person. He incorporates in himself the powers of an Islamic seer, the knowledge of the sorcerer, and the machinations of the witch-doctor.

Witchcraft remains a world taken for granted lingering in the subconscious of many Africans and surfacing in times of crises such as sudden death, motor accidents,and childlessness.[22] If the independent African churches have become so popular and are growing by leaps and bounds,[23] their popularity is largely due to the claim of such movements to be endowed with the power to eradicate and successfully destroy the powers of witchcraft. The traditional churches in Africa, including the Catholic Church, stand to lose if they do not take up ritual and theological arms against the myriads of elemental spirits inhabiting the African world.

The urgent task of the African theologian is to see to it that his African brothers and sisters are not made prey of "by philosophy and empty deceit, according to human tradition, according to the elemental spirits of the universe" (Col 2:8). Even though political or revolutionary theology may end with the acquisition of the political rights,the social reforms, the economic readjustments, and the cultural rejuvenation of once-despised African cultures, the theology that liberates man from the elemental spirits and orients him to Christ, the only Savior, remains a lasting reality. For the elemental spirits show their ugly heads in different forms according to different times and seasons, thus making prey of all and sundry.

An African theology based only on culture and inculturation will speak meaningfully to Africans all right, but will it have a universal value? Black Theology tends to redress the apartheid system of South Africa and the discrimination of persons according to the colour of their skin, but does Black Theology not tend to be a ghetto theology? In any event an African Theology of total liberation, with special emphasis on liberation from the elemental spirits and witchcraft, should be a permanent and enviable theological contribution not just for Africa but for the rest of the world.

Paul Bemile

NOTES

1. John S. Pobee, *Toward an African Theology* (Nashville: 1979), 18.
2. A number of participants at the Annual Conference of the West African Association of the Theological Institutions held at Ibadan, Nigeria, in August 1976, openly expressed scepticism about evolving an African theology. The present writer was an eye-witness. The proceedings of this meeting were mimeographed by the then Secretary, Edward W. Fasholé-Luke and distributed to the member Institutions.
3. R. Sastre, "Liturgie Romaine at Nègritude," in *Des Prêtres Noirs S'interrogent,* (Paris, 1957), p. 163, wrote even before The Second Vatican Council: "Adaptation is not particularisation of the universal, if I may refer to it thus, but the elevation of the particular to a universal resonance. Particularism would mean finding value only in what originates from oneself or from one's own people. Alienation, on the other hand, is to be incapable of finding among one's own people anything that could possibly have a universal vocation."
4. Cf. AAS 61 (1961) 577.
5. Cf. AAS 61 (1961) 578.
6. Cited according to Aylward Shorter, *African Christian Theology—Adaptation or Incarnation?* (New York: Maryknoll, 1977), 23.
7. John S. Pobee, *Towards an African Theology*, 22.
8. W.E. Abraham, *The Mind of Africa,* (London: 1962), 46. In this book the former Pro-Vice Chancellor of the University of Ghana, expresses his belief that family resemblance in Africa makes the treatment of one tribe, in this case, the Akan people of Ghana, necessarily say something about all African cultures.
9. E. Bolaji Odowu, *African Traditional Religion: A Definition* (London: 1973), 106.
10. Cf. *The Historical Study of African Religion,* ed. T.O. Ranger and I Kimambo (London: 1972); Shorter, *African Christian Theology,* 50ff.
11. E.E.Y. Evans-Pritchard, *Nuer Religion* (Oxford: 1956).
12. R.G. Lienhardt, *Divinity and Experience: The Religion of the Dinka* (Oxford: 1961).
13. R.P. Girault, "Essai sur la Religion des Dagara," *Bull. IFAN* 21(1959), 329–356, especially 331.
14. J. Goody, *The Myth of the Bagre* (Oxford: 1972), 29 ff.
15. Germaine Dieterlen, "Contribution à l'étude des relations protohistoriques entre le Mande et l'actuel Ghana," *Vacamonica Symposium 1972—Actes du Symposium International sur les religions de prèhistoire,* 18–23, Septembre 1972, ed. Emmanuel Anati,

(Capo di Ponte Brescia: 1975), 367–378.

16. Dieterlen, *Le Mande et l'actuel Ghana*, 376.
17. R. Mauny, "Tableau geographique de l'Afrique de l'Ouest au Moyen-Age, d'apres les sources écrites, la tradition et l'archéologie," *Memoire de l'IFAN* 61 (Dakar: 1961); Dieterlen, *Le Mande et l'actuel Ghana*, 367.
18. Shorter, *African Christian Theology*, 61–77, for East Africa; Goody, *Myth of the Bagre*, 25–27, for West Africa. See also J.S. Mbiti, *Concepts of God in Africa*, (London: 1970), 327–336, for the list of African peoples, their countries, and God names.
19. Cf. *Theologen der dritten Welt*, 96.
20. Allan Aubrey Boesak, *Unschuld, die schuldig macht: Eine sozial-ethische Studie uber Schwarze Theologie und Schwarze Macht* (Hamburg: 1977), 31; see also A.A. Boesak, "The Crucified Christ Challenges the Powers of the World: South Africa," *International Review of Mission* 69 (1980): 342–344.
21. Allan Aubrey Boesak, "The Black Church and the Struggle in South Africa," *The Ecumenical Review* 32 (1980), 23.
22. John S. Pobee, *Toward an African Theology*, 49.
23. Cf. C.G. Baeta, *Prophetism in Ghana: A Study of some "Spiritual" Churches* (London: 1962).

Shepherd of His Flock

Jesus said to Peter a third time: 'Simon, son of John, do you love me?' Peter was upset that he asked him the third time, 'Do you love me?' and said, 'Lord, you know everything, you know I love you.' Jesus said to him, 'Feed my sheep.'

(Jn 21:17)

This conversation took place between Jesus and Simon Peter around the year A.D. 33, on the shores of the sea of Tiberias.

About one thousand nine hundred and twenty-six years later, to be more precise, in 1959, a similar conversation took place between the Vicar of Christ, Pope John XXIII, and another Peter. The Pope was looking for a shepherd to look after his flock in the new Diocese of Wa, which he was about to create. He came across a tall, sharp-eyed, jovial, and dynamic young priest, called Peter Dery, in the Savannah land of the Upper West, and asked him: "Peter, son of Poreku, are you willing to shepherd God's flock in the new ecclesiastical territory of the Upper West that I am about to create?"

Dery was perplexed, but he said: "Yes, I am." And so he was nominated shepherd of God's sheep in the Wa Diocese on 3 November 1959.

I: DERY LEADS HIS FLOCK

Having given his irrevocable "yes" to the Pope, Dery made up his mind not to take his appointment lightly but to put his whole heart into the task. On 8 May 1960, in the basilica of St. Peter the Apostle, he was anointed and commissioned to lead the flock in the Diocese of Wa by the prestigious Pope John XXIII. Strengthened by the Holy Spirit, Dery returned to Wa on 11 June 1960, and took full responsibility of his flock. His task was to feed this flock with the word of God, with the sacraments and, indeed, with everything that makes man whole. He knew the Pope did not appoint him to look after souls only but after integral human beings and to lead them to God their Father.

1. Liturgical inculturation

Dery's first concern was to make the Christian religion meaningful to his flock. Christian life, even though enthusiastically embraced by the people, was still new and certain aspects of it seemed strange to them. Dery knew, even before Vatican II said it, that the liturgy is the source and the summit of the Christian life. This being so, the liturgy must be celebrated in such a way that it meets the deepest aspirations of the flock. In other words, it must so harmonize with their mentality and religious values that they feel at home in it. Consequently, Dery undertook an intensive liturgical renewal in his new Diocese. Fortunately for him, the young diocese had not fallen victim to the diehard liturgical traditions that met with strong resistance to Vatican II's liturgical renewal in many places. No sooner then was Dery installed as bishop than he requested from Rome the permission to translate the "Ordinary" of the Mass into Dagare and have it sung in local melodies, accompanied by local musical instruments. Permission was granted, and Dery himself composed the first Dagare mass. It became a milestone in the process of Africanisation of the Church in Ghana. He composed other hymns, including litanies of the Saints and of the Blessed Virgin Mary, which are still very much in use today.

Under his leadership, almost all the sacramental rites have been translated and adapted to suit local conditions. Words that had deep religious meaning for the people but were considered unbecoming by the missionaries because they were "pagan," found their way back into the Christian liturgy and catechesis, thus becoming Christianized. Words like *Bagre* (sacrifice), *maal bagre* (to sacrifice), *Bare koo* (pour libation), *Bagmaala* (sacrificer, priest), *Kpeen* (ancestor), *Ngmen* (spirit), *Kontoma* (satan), *Dapare* (heaven, home of ancestors), *Dazugo vuu* (home of the wicked) have gained back their natural place and use in Christian doctrine and worship, without in any way adulterating the purity of the Christian religion.

Ever since Dery lit that torch of liturgical renewal in the Diocese of Wa, it has never been extinguished. Today one can honestly say that the Diocese of Wa is the most advanced in the process of liturgical renewal and inculturation in the whole country. Because Dery is a pastor to the marrow, the need of his flock to worship God with all that it has and all that it possesses takes precedence before rubrics and doctrinal orthodoxy.

2. Laity Involvement

From the outset, Dery was acutely aware of the fact that the Church of Christ is not the Church of the clergy alone, but principally of the laity. The Church is missioned to sow the Word of God, which is like a seed in the world. But in order that the seed may grow, the farm has to be cultivated. The laity can be said to be the cultivators in the world. The clergy has the duty to nourish them and provide them with the seed for sowing. If the farm is not cultivated, no seed can be grown, let alone grow.

Understanding the Church in this manner, Dery knew that this portion of it that is now entrusted to him cannot be effective in its evangelising activities without the active involvement of the laity. How was this to be realized when the laity has been taught that his role in the Church is to pay, pray, and obey? This is a far cry from active involvement. Indeed, at the time Dery became the spiritual leader of Wa Diocese, and even today, the position of the laity in the Church could be compared favourably to a trip in a bus. First, there is the bus owner who may also be its driver. His duty is to see to it that the bus is in a good travelling condition, able to reach its destination. Connected with the bus but not owning it, are the "bookmen" or ticket sellers whose duty it is to sell tickets to passengers and make sure that the bus is full. Then there are the passengers who, though important, enjoy only a passive role after buying their ticket. They simply have to secure a seat in the bus and sit down calmly to be driven to their destination.

The parable is easy to interpret. The bus is the Church. Its owners are the bishops and priests, the ticket sellers are the catechists, and the passengers are the laity. The destination is heaven.

With this image in the minds of many people, it is not surprising that they maintain their membership in the Church only as a means of going to heaven. Such an understanding of the Church is very unhealthy. The Church was established by Christ to be a leaven in the world, and every Christian must consider himself as leaven to leaven, as light to enlighten, and as salt to season his/her world.

Dery worked hard to give the right image of the Church to his flock. When he took over the diocese, there was one organized lay movement, namely the Legion of Mary. Only a small fraction of the laity was in this movement. The youth involvement in it was negligible. What then was the vast majority of the laity doing in the Church? How was Christ and his good news to be preached if the Christians saw their role to consist only in the performance of their religious duties, the consumption of the sacraments, and the stocking up of merit for heaven?

The young men meanwhile drifted to the cities in search of lucrative employments and the young girls sat and waited to get married and become house-wives. Dery saw that this state of affairs was very unhealthy in a young local church and needed to be changed. He set out to organize, train, and involve all the Christians in the lay apostolate. First, he launched a crusade of retreats for the various groups of Christians: young girls, young boys, adult women, and adult men. It was a crushing task, but it was worth it, for it yielded the desired results: active participation of the laity in the life of the Church.

Catholic Action Groups of boys, girls, men, and women began to emerge in every parish and outstation. They were trained to use the "See-Judge-Act" method to study their own environment and with the light of the Gospel improve the situation. The Dagare woman who has always been suppressed in the male-dominated Dagare society learnt, for the first time, to speak boldly in public, in front of men. It was a liberation that hitherto was undreamed of. Girls gained self-confidence and asserted themselves when they needed to. Catholic Action leaders shoot up like mushrooms in every part of the diocese, actively engaged in the apostolate, ready to make any sacrifice for the Gospel. Dery had struck the dormant chords in the hearts of many Christians and made them not only hearers of the Word but doers as well (Jas 1:22).

Human development

As mentioned above, Dery understood his mission to consist not only in the care of souls but in the redemption of every aspect of human life, for human beings do not only have spiritual needs, but bodily, intellectual, and social needs as well. The good pastor cannot neglect any of these needs without harm to his flock. Dery's flock was, by nature, good, obedient, and hard working, but it was often beset by poverty, disease, and ignorance. The institutions set up by the missionaries to combat these evils, namely education, health services, and economic development, had to be consolidated and expanded. Dery threw his full weight on this task. As other writers are likely to speak of Dery's leadership in education and health services, I shall limit my observations to his endeavours in the socioeconomic development programmes, especially in the field of credit unions.

When Dery became the shepherd of Wa Diocese, the seed of the credit union movement had already been planted in Jirapa, but the young plant seemed to be facing a dramatic drought, for it could not grow up fast. Soon after he arrived, Dery started to water the credit union plant, and very quickly it shot up and spread its branches to all the parishes. He established a systematic programme for the training of the officers of the movement. The most brilliant of them were sent to the University of St. Francis Xavier in Antigonish, Canada, for further training. Within a short time, Wa Diocese became the cradle and the champion of credit unionism in Ghana. Today there are over twenty credit union primary societies in the Upper West, with a capital savings of over $20 million.

One cannot but feel proud of such an achievement,

not only because of the incredibly high savings accumulated from such a reputedly poor region, but more because of the economic education it has brought to the people. They have learnt to save their little earnings with the credit union instead of burying it in the ground or in the rafters where it used to serve as delicious meals for the termites and rats.

4. Vocation Promotion

When Dery took possession of his new diocese, there were only four diocesan priests and six major seminarians, besides the less than twenty White Fathers serving in the diocese. The Franciscan Missionaries of Mary (FMM), the White Sisters (WS), and the Sisters of Mary Immaculate (SMI) had few houses in the diocese. The Brothers of St. Joseph, which was started by the White Fathers to receive indigenous young men into the Brotherhood and to the religious life, was passing through a period of uncertainty. This was all that Dery had as co-workers in the Lord's vineyard.

As the diocese, from the day of its erection, was entrusted to the local clergy, Dery quickly realized that, if he was to do a good job and have continuity in his work, he must recruit more people into the clergy and the religious life from among the local people. This was no challenge to Dery, for even as a seminarian, he drew many boys to follow in his footsteps. He has a charisma for attracting the youth. He only needed to intensify and accelerate what he was already doing in the field of vocation promotion. In 1963, he opened his own junior seminary, St. Francis Xavier, at Wa, and continued to be in close contact with students of St. Charles Junior Seminary, and other students who showed interest in the priesthood. The number of major seminarians steadily swelled up to very encouraging proportions. When he left Wa in 1975, after fifteen years of pontificate, the number of Diocesan priests had moved from four to thirty, of which two died. There were also many major seminarians. This is a great achievement when one considers the length of time spent in the training of a priest, and also the fact that many drop off on the way.

In 1965, through the instrumentality of Dery, the Brothers of the Immaculate Conception (FIC), a teaching congregation, arrived in Wa to take charge of the training of the Brothers in Kaleo, who were known as the Brothers of St. Joseph. The FIC decided to absorb them into their congregation, as they could not train brothers different from themselves. Those who opted to join them were absorbed into the FIC society. The arrival of the FIC in the diocese opened a new era in vocational education in the Upper West.

Much as I would have loved to elaborate on this aspect of the Brothers' work, I am afraid I shall have to leave it to those writers who are dealing with Dery's educational leadership. Suffice it to say as a conclusion to this paragraph that the arrival of the FIC through Dery ushered in a new dimension of Christian living, namely men religious. Today the number of African members of the Institute in the region has exceeded that of the Dutch and Indonesian members, and there are many serious young men who seek to join them. They are very cautious in selecting them, because they want to lay a solid foundation for a truly active religious life. Though the Institute is basically a teaching congregation, some of its members are engaged in various apostolates, like construction, catechetics, the prisons, etc. We owe a big gratitude to Dery for bringing them into Ghana.

Dery did not only recruit boys and girls for the priesthood and the religious life. He also made sure that the more capable ones among them received further training besides the initial formation they received in the seminary and the noviciate, so that he had the right person for the right job, at the right time, in the pastoral ministry. Of twenty-eight diocesan priests of his time, seven were sent to do further studies in various disciplines for specific service in the country. Indeed, all of them are now strategically placed in various areas, from teaching in the universities and seminaries to running a diocese. Dery's foresight is paying dividends.

II: DERY HEADS ANOTHER FLOCK

By 1970, after Dery had toiled for ten years to lead his flock in the green pastures of the Lord, the signs of the burden of pastoral care were beginning to show in Dery's physical stature. His strong and straight shoulders had given way to a slight bend, grey locks of hair were appearing on his head, and his sportive gait was dampening. Though Dery was at the peak of success, he would not rest on his laurels. Painstakingly he went on, always endeavouring to bring his flock closer to the Chief Shepherd, Jesus Christ.

It was around this time that rumours started circulating that Dery was likely to be transferred to head another flock. These rumours waxed fat when Dery was appointed Apostolic Administrator of Tamale Diocese in 1972 after the resignation of the Rt. Rev. Gabriel W. Champagne, W.F., Bishop of Tamale, for reasons of ill health. In January 1975 Dery received a letter from the Holy See on which was printed *sub secreto pontificio* (Top Vatican Secret). The secret was an open one, for everyone knew by then that Dery was going to be transferred to Tamale as its Bishop.

In the letter Pope Paul VI asked Dery a similar question that John XXIII had asked him: "Peter, son of Poreku, are you willing to leave your beloved flock that you cherish so much in the Wa Diocese to shepherd a different flock?"

It was hard, but Dery again said, "Yes, I am," for he is not a man who sticks stingily to his achievements. So in March 1975 Dery left Wa to take charge of God's flock in the Diocese of Tamale. Two years later, that is, in 1977, Dery was raised to the rank of Archbishop in the Roman Catholic Church, with Navrongo/Bolgatanga and his former see of Wa as his suffragans.

Dery's zeal as shepherd has never been dampened by this painful transfer. He continued to exercise the same pastoral concern for his new flock, which had a different background. One achievement in Dery's new diocese deserves special mention. When he took over the direction of the Tamale Diocese in 1975, there was not a single diocesan priest nor major seminarian. At the time of writing, the Diocese of Tamale has eight diocesan priests and eighteen major seminarians.

III. DERY THE GOOD SHEPHERD

We shall now devote a few lines to speak of Dery's personality as a shepherd. In John 10:11–16, our Lord Jesus Christ tells us what qualities a shepherd must have in order to be a good shepherd: knowledge of the sheep; love for and commitment to the sheep. How does Dery tally with these qualities?

Dery certainly knows his sheep. He knows them not just as a flock but individually as well. It would, of course, be a miracle for anyone to know individually the names of 520,000 people scattered over an area of eight thousand square miles. All the same, Dery did know quite a lot of people among his flock. He has a great capacity for retaining names of people in his memory. He knows many young people through the physical features of their parents or grandparents, or through the resemblance of a brother or sister.

As Dery knows his sheep, so do the sheep know him. This I can testify from my own experience. Even today, nine years after I have succeeded Dery as the Bishop of Wa, many still call me Bishop Dery. Several times it happened to me on my treks that shepherds would jump out of the bush and greet: "Yaane, Bishop Dery." (Greetings, Bishop Dery). Once a cousin of mine brought her daughter who claimed to have missed me because she had not seen me for a long time. The young girl was beaming with smiles when she approached me and greeted me fondly.

Then I asked, "Do you know me?"

"Of course, I know you." she answered.

"Who am I?" I insisted.

"You are Bishop Dery!" she replied.

A good shepherd does not only know his sheep but loves them and cares for them. The best proof of love of any person or of anything is the willingness to give one's time, nay, one's life to that person or thing, "for there can be no greater love than the man who is ready to die for his friends," (Jn 15:13). Dery's whole time was spent for his flock. In all his years of shepherdhood in Wa, I never heard once that Dery was on holidays. Genuine love manifests itself especially in moments of sickness, disasters, difficulties, and loss. Dery was always sympathetic to those sheep in the flock who were victims in these situations and offered the necessary help, material or spiritual. Someone once remarked to me: *"Bishop Dery nang wul doo nga faä neezaa kong la bang wul'o."* (Since

Bishop Dery has failed to correct this man, nobody can help him.)

A good shepherd will look for the lost sheep: For as Jesus puts it: "What man among you with a hundred sheep, losing one, would not leave the ninety-nine in the wilderness and go after the missing one till he found it?" (Lk 15:4).

Dery literally went after his lost sheep till he found them. I still remember the story of how Dery went after the runaway wife of one of the Christians. This man reported to Dery that his wife had "run away" from him, and news had reached him that she was living with a pagan in a village twenty-five miles from Wa. Dery quickly summoned his driver, and within minutes they were tearing down the dusty road to the village. When they arrived, Dery and the driver stayed in the car some few hundred yards away from the house while the husband inspected the house. Seeing that the woman was not in the house, the man mounted guard on a tree and they waited. As if driven by an unknown power, the woman returned shortly from the bush and entered the house. Having spotted the bishop's car as she entered the house, she guessed that there was something afoot. She quickly repaired into the darkest room in the house and hid herself under the *bugo* (grain storage built of clay).

The husband came down from the tree and stood by the house while Dery and the driver went in and asked, "Where is the woman that has just entered the house?"

"Woman! We haven't seen any woman enter this house."

"If you don't show me the woman right now, you'll be sorry for it," Dery emphasized. Seeing the authority and determination in his face, they knew at once that they were not dealing with some kind of weak person.

They led him into the dark room and there was the woman, coiled up like a python under the "Bugo." Dery brought the woman out and drove her back to Wa where, after a serious admonition, he restored her to the husband.

Dedication and commitment are two high qualities of a good shepherd, for as Christ says: "The good shepherd is one who lays down his life for his sheep, whereas the hired hand, since he is not the shepherd and the sheep do not belong to him, abandons the sheep and runs away as soon as he sees a wolf coming (cf. Jn 10:11–12). Dery was totally committed to his sheep. He has never been known to give in to wolves threatening to drive him away from his sheep. What are the wolves that are likely to distract Christ's shepherds from their sheep? There are four ferocious wolves that often pose as threats to Christ's shepherd: Fame, Wealth, Woman, and the Bottle. Dery has never given way to any of these wolves, hence his flock has never suffered from the absence of its shepherd. Dery is so dedicated to his work that he does not even notice the presence of wolves.

Dery does not do things by halves. When he works, he works, when he eats, he eats, and when he sleeps, he sleeps. He always enjoys a good bowl of *saab* (Dagaba staple food), with plenty of meat (*Jutajuta*). But who would not, after exerting himself so unsparingly day in and day out? Dery's sonorous sleeps indicate that he sleeps well, and that is probably what keeps him going.

When Dery gives a homily, the average time is fifty minutes. The underlying principle is the same: thoroughness in what you do. There is the story that on one Christmas Day, in order to avoid Dery's long homily in the cathedral, a group of people left Wa to attend mass at one of the neighbouring parishes. To their utter amazement and embarrassment, they discovered that Dery was the principal celebrant of that mass. They were caught in their own scheme and deserved to be preached to, and Dery gave it to them for at least fifty minutes.

CONCLUSION: What I have written in this brief article can only reflect in a very small way the active pastoral life of Archbishop Dery. Indeed Dery possesses such a remarkably rich personality as a pastor that it is impossible to do full justice to his pastoral ministry in so short an article.

Dery's motto, which you can read on his Coat of Arms, is: *"Apostolus Jesu Christi"* (Apostle of Jesus Christ). This is what he has tried to be in all his twenty-five years of spiritual leadership: a true Apostle of the Lord Jesus Christ and of His Flock.

G.E. Kpiebaya

Towards Effective Youth Movement: A Sociological Viewpoint

This article is dedicated to a man who, throughout his life, has demonstrated sustained dedicated commitment to the integral welfare and development of the youth of this land: PETER POREKUU DERY, Catholic Archbishop of Tamale, Ghana.

INTRODUCTION

The youth, it is generally recognized, have the potential of influencing the flow and ebb of societal life. This centrality of the youth is amply evidenced by the U.N. declaration of 1985 as the International Year of the Youth. This short paper is an attempt to contribute to the ongoing discussions on, and deliberations about the youth. Indeed, it is the direct outgrowth of a recently completed nationwide evaluative research on the youth and Church in Ghana (unpublished as of now), a research in which the present writer made a painstaking analysis of the dimensions of religiosity of Catholic Youth, the nature and extent of youth social problems, and the extent to which the various Church youth movements or associations have been effective. It is the intention of the present paper to present a theoretical model on effective youth movement, a model that is applicable to various types and styles of youth organizations. It is to examine the structural and behavioural properties of youth associations that can be instrumental towards their effectiveness. First, conceptualization.

YOUTH MOVEMENTS AS VOLUNTARY FORMAL ORGANIZATIONS

The concepts youth movements, youth associations, and youth organizations will be used interchangeably throughout this paper. An organization emerges when explicit procedures are established to coordinate the activities of people in the interest of achieving specific objectives. It implies the rational coordination of the activities of a number of people for the achievement of some common explicit purpose or goal. Youth movements are, by definition, voluntary associations. Voluntary associations are formal groups organized for specialized and specifically stated purpose. Certain common interests exist among its members. Membership is based on deliberate choice, however. Otherwise stated, voluntary youth organizations are behaviour systems or systems of action that have a definite organization of goals towards which activities of group members are oriented. Perceptible effective youth movement is thus to be measured by the extent to which goals of association are realized, that is, the actual translation into reality of the defined objectives of the organization. This is functionally related to several intragroup and intergroup attributes.

ASSOCIATION AS ACTORS

Youth movements or organizations have an inherent importance of their own (Mouzelis, 1972). They serve in society as a whole as arenas within which new ideas are generated. They are communication networks through which people may learn and form attitudes about important areas of life. They serve as means of training potential leaders in the skills not only of the apostolate, but in politics also. They serve as places in which members can attain the status necessary to become leaders. They exist as one of the principal means of getting individuals to participate in the larger social arena, and they create a forum for forming a critical outlook on important social and political issues. Youth associations, therefore, form the needed environment for molding and transforming the individual human raw material into a mature person, capable of playing a responsible social role. As such, they constitute one of the most crucial conditions for generating effectiveness both in youth movement and youth development.

Youth movements are a specific type of human action (Parsons and Shils, 1951). There is a structure to every rational human action. The act consists of the actor, the goal, and the orientation. The actor is the agent. It can be an individual, like an editor requesting papers for a journal. The actor can also be a collectivity or a group of people, like the GHANCYC (Ghana National Catholic Youth Council), presenting an objectively critical position paper on the socio-political problems facing the country. The orientation of the actor embraces the alternative means that the actor selects within the specific environment to realize certain well-defined goals. The goals represent the end, the purpose, and the ultimate term of the action. These three elements of action would feature were a group of Y.C.S.—Young Christian Students—(Actor) to spend a whole day educating a rural population (orientation) on the importance of organizing village consumer cooperatives (goal).

The various Catholic youth organizations—GHANCYC, YCS, Pax Romana, Aquinas Societies, Young Christian Workers, etc.—are actors. Seen in this light, these organizations obtain not a static but a dynamic character.

They are formal organizations because they are units of action and interaction—systems of action—that have a definite orientation to well-defined goals. If goals are to be realized, considerable amount of human behaviour has to be channelized and directed towards their realization. Patterned channelization of human behaviour towards felt goals generates and maintains group cohesion, group support for policies and objectives, and group identification. It is obvious that this in turn increases group morale, which enhances effectiveness (Price, 1971).

These Catholic Youth Organizations operate as systems of action with a goal-achievement orientation. They are systems that utilize energy (given up by humans) in a directed effort to alter the condition of human basic material in a determined way. They produce something by adding a value to human objects through altering them, and in return receive resources from their environment. They alter the human material by transmitting values and attitudes. Attitudes are not transmitted by birth; neither are they inherited. Rather they are learned and acquired in the process of interaction with other actors. Attitude formation and attitude change in terms of the gospel value system is at the core of the youth movements. It attempts as its primary task, to alter the state of attitudes and values, thereby producing a quality person. Indeed, the broad and crucial objective of these associations is to provide and develop among young people a personal faith in God, and to promote and develop opportunities for its members to respond to that faith, to reach greater maturity to respond to that faith, to reach greater maturity in the likeness and life-style of Jesus Christ as well as to provide processes for Christian growth. Hence one of the criteria on which effective youth movements can be judged is whether or not and to what extent these broad goals have been objectivized. They provide the yardstick on which effectiveness can be measured. It can be stated that the more these stated goals are realized, the greater the effectiveness of the youth movements, and vice versa.

But the objectivation of these official goals is contingent on what can be termed operative goals, that is, the actions and interactions that characterize the functioning of the groups themselves as ongoing systems. It is these operative goals that constitute the means or orientation for goal achievement and, therefore, effectiveness of any organization. It is these that constitute the generating conditions for effectiveness of youth movements. Stated differently, for youth movements to be effective, certain basic properties have to be present within youth organisations themselves, properties that relate to their structure and functioning.

OPEN SYSTEMS

If youth apostolate is to be effective, then youth associations need to be open systems. This concept is already present in our previous affirmation that youth movements take place within a definite socio-cultural context. As opposed to closed systems, which are independent, self-contained units, an open system is vitally aware of its limitations or its dependence on, and relationship with its environment. Problems of relationships, of structure, of interdependence have to be dealt with. Youth movements as living, open systems, need to exhibit a growth or expansion that is dynamic, that maximizes their basic character. This growth can be qualitative, that is, in terms of self-transformation; it can be quantitative in terms of numerical expansion. Both qualitative and quantitative expansions are necessary if optimal effectiveness is to be realized in terms of goal-achievement. Stated differently, effectiveness will be contingent on the ability of these associations to survive, to maintain their characteristic internal order, and to import new energy from their environment in terms of inducting new actors into the associations.

Of crucial importance is feedback system. The feedback principle has to do with information input, which is a kind of signal to the association about general conditions, and about the functioning of the system in relation to other functioning systems—political, economic, cultural, and social. The feedback of such information enables the system to correct for its own malfunctioning or for changes in the environment and thus to maintain a steady state of balance. This is a dynamic rather than a static balance, however. Youth associations being open systems, are not to be at rest but should tend towards differentiation and elaboration because of the relationship between growth and survival. Furthermore they should be able to reach the same objective from different initial conditions and by different paths of development. Thus for effectiveness to result, youth associations will have to have a dynamic interaction with their total environment.

Effectiveness is likewise a function of the internal system of the group. Indeed, this appears to be a crucial determining factor. The actual operation of the group, the lines of action and interaction. The degree of identification with, commitment to the group ideals, and competent functional enlightened leadership; these constitute elements that either generate or stifle effectiveness, enhance or inhibit it.

AUTONOMY

It appears that a relationship exists between group autonomy and effective operation of the group. Autonomy relates to a significant control of the association by its members. It refers to the ability of group members to significantly control the structure and functioning of the group. It relates to the ability of group members to engage in innovative thinking, initiate programmes, and execute them. It also concerns the ability of membership to critically assess and evaluate the group in terms of its past, and its orientation towards the future. Autonomy, however, demands dedicated, enlightened leadership, a leadership competent enough to ably contain and direct the flow and ebb of the group life. It likewise requires responsible membership, which is vitally aware that the destiny and life of the group is its responsibility. All other things being equal, the more autonomous an organization, the more the likelihood that it will be effective; the less autonomous an organization, the less the likelihood that it will be effective.

TASK ORIENTATION

It was observed by Karl Marx that philosophers have so far, merely reflected or meditated on the world; what is needed, however, is that the world should be transformed. For any measurable effectiveness to result, an organization has to be task-oriented. It has to systematically and critically analyze the situation, prescribe solutions to problems, and actually execute the prescription. An organization that operates merely at the analytic level will not be effective in any meaningful sense. Analysis will have to give birth to action if significant results are to accrue. Involvement in concrete tasks generates and maintains group life. For if the group members interact frequently, then the degree of their liking for one another will very likely increase, and vice versa; otherwise stated, the more frequently group members interact with one another, the more alike in some respects both their activities and their sentiments tend to become (Homans, 1950). Similarity begets liking and interaction; these in turn will beget more similarity; this begets additional liking and interaction, which in turn begets more similarity, and so on, and so forth. The end result of this process would be the creation of consciousness on the part of group members that they belong to the group. The group becomes then a reference point for the behaviour of individual group members. It creates identification with group goals and ideals, and philosophy. It also creates and/or increases group cohesion and morale. The potential for effectiveness of these group properties is simply overwhelming.

LEADERSHIP

Ultimately leadership plays a role of central importance in group effectiveness. The life of the collectivity depends on the type and quality of leadership. Leaders can transform a group into a very sharp instrument for achievement; they can also turn it into a blunt, useless, dead object. Leadership is not an end in itself. Many organizations expire or become transformed into oligarchies simply because leaders might view leadership status as an end in itself rather than as means to an end. Leadership is service; it is the soul of the organization. Dedicated and committed membership depends largely on dedicated

and committed leadership. The level of membership conformity to group norms depends to a very great extent on
the degree to which leaders conform to group norms.
Group cohesion and morale are end-products of leadership. After all, it is leadership that channelizes the behaviour of individuals towards felt group goals; it is
leadership that stimulates and encourages innovative
thinking and, in the final analysis, acts as a catalyst for
the effective functioning of the group. One might maintain, then, that the soul of the various youth associations
resides in the quality of leadership that operates within
them. Effective youth association is largely a product of
effective, dedicated, committed leadership.

SUMMARY

Summarily stated, this short paper attempts to locate
effective youth movement within the group context. It
sees the various Catholic youth movements as voluntary
formal associations with specific goals towards which the
behaviour of group members is rationally channelized in
a patterned, consistent manner. These associations are
powerful milieux within which solid persons can be
moulded with potential for articulate leadership. The social processes among individuals and leaders are of central importance for the realization of group objectives.
Stated differently, it is in the smooth interaction of all
these group elements among themselves, and between
them and the total environment that group life is given
birth to, and can be kept throbbing.

It is thus manifestly clear that the members of the
various youth organizations are, at the same time, both
the primary producers of the product and its consumers.
The intended product of the youth movement is the crea-

tion of persons imbued with the spirit of the gospel, and capable of invading their particular socio-cultural environments with the same spirit. The ability to effectively penetrate and perfect the social milieu in a healthy way will depend on the extent to which the actor/agent is himself imbued with, and perfected by the spirit of the gospel. Hence the primary product of youth movement would be to transform the youth themselves by altering them, by adding some values to them as persons. Groups have the potential of transforming individuals; individuals form groups. There is thus a two-way interaction between the group and the individual; they are interdependent; they influence and are influenced by each other. It is thus abundantly clear that effective youth movement is both a group product and an individual responsibility. It is contingent on individuals who have been effectively transformed; it is likewise a product of formal youth organizations or associations that have, as their ultimate objective, the creation of a new man and a new social order characterised by honesty, freedom, social justice, and dedicated and committed social participation. To the extent to which these lofty ideals and objectives are actualized, to that extent only are youth movements effective.

Yvon Yangyuoru

References

Homans, George C. *The Human Group*. New York: Harcourt, Brace, & World, Inc., 1950.

Mouzelis, Nicol, P. *Organization and Bureaucracy*. Chicago: Aldine, Atherton, 1972.

Parsons, Talcott, and Shils, Edward A. *Toward a General Theory of Action*. New York: Harper and Row, 1951.

Price, James L. *Organizational Effectiveness*. Homewood, Illinois: Richard D. Irwin, Inc., 1971.